INTERPRETING THE OLD TESTAMENT

INTERPRETING
THE OLD TESTAMENT
A Practical Guide

Daniel J. Harrington, S.J.

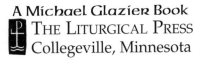

A Michael Glazier Book
THE LITURGICAL PRESS
Collegeville, Minnesota

A Michael Glazier Book published by The Liturgical Press

Cover design by Ann Blattner. Photo of the Sinai Desert by Hugh Witzmann, O.S.B.

Originally published as Volume 1 of the *Old Testament Message* series, Carroll Stuhlmueller, C.P., and Martin McNamara, M.S.C., editors.

	11	12	13	14	15	16

Library of Congress Cataloging-in-Publication Data

Harrington, Daniel J.
    Interpreting the Old Testament : a practical guide / Daniel J. Harrington.
       p. cm. — (The Message of biblical spirituality ; v. 1)
    "A Michael Glazier book."
    Reprint. Originally published: Wilmington, Del. : M. Glazier, © 1981. (Old Testament message ; v. 1).
    Includes bibliographical references.
    ISBN 0-8146-5236-0
    1. Bible. O.T.—Introductions. 2. Bible. O.T.—Criticism, interpretation, etc. I. Title. II. Series. III. Series: Old Testament message ; v. 1.
BS1140.2.H317   1991
221.6'1—dc20   91-3385
                                            CIP

Contents

INTERPRETING THE OLD TESTAMENT

INTRODUCTION

THE SECOND VATICAN COUNCIL'S Dogmatic Constitution on Divine Revelation (section 12) insists that biblical interpreters investigate the meaning that the sacred writers intended to express. It goes on to state that due attention should be paid to the customs followed in biblical times and to the prevailing styles of perceiving, speaking, and narrating. This introduction to Old Testament exegesis responds to those directives and provides readers of the *Old Testament Message* series with an initiation into the methods commonly used in biblical scholarship today. It is designed for beginners, and so it presents mainline positions and avoids the novel and idiosyncratic.

This book should be read along with my contribution to the *New Testament Message* series, *Interpreting the New Testament: A Practical Guide* (1979; 2nd ed., 1981). The format of the two volumes is quite similar. Each chapter explains a method used in biblical studies, illustrates the method by a few examples, and offers about ten suggestions for further study. In view of what is contained in the previous book, I felt less obligation to proceed so methodically in laying bare the logic involved in each method. I also saw no need to repeat the sections on using several translations, the history of interpretation, the interpreter's presuppositions, and exegesis and spirituality. But the importance of these matters for Old Testament exegesis should not be ignored.

In addition to explaining the tried and true approaches to Old Testament interpretation, this book provides information that is needed for an intelligent use of the commentaries in the series. It discusses some of the major moments in ancient Israel's religious tradition: Abraham and Isaac, the escape from Egypt, the Sinai covenant, the call of Gideon, the promise to David, the destruction of the Jerusalem temple, the return from exile, and the rebuilding of the temple. Special emphasis is placed on the themes of God's relationship with his people and the tradition of faith. These two themes emerge quite sharply from both the methods of interpretation and the examples used to illustrate them.

I dedicate this book to the memory of my late father, Florence Daniel Harrington. The invitation to write it was the topic of our last conversation on the evening before his very sudden death. He showed great interest in the book and in the series, as he had previously in *Interpreting the New Testament* and the *New Testament Message* series. The central themes of this book—God's relationship with his people and the Old Testament as expressing the tradition of faith—were things that he taught me in oblique and often unconscious ways through many years.

Daniel J. Harrington, S.J.

1. BASIC LITERARY CRITICISM

A. The Old Testament as Literature

A BROWSER, who enters the religion section in a bookstore or library and pages through the various editions of the Bible, will probably come away confused by the experience. If the browser first picks up a translation of the Bible prepared under Jewish auspices or even a copy of the Hebrew Bible, there will be twenty-four books separated into three major divisions. The Torah or Law consists of the books of Genesis, Exodus, Leviticus, Numbers, and Deuteronomy. The Prophets contain Joshua, Judges, 1–2 Samuel, 1–2 Kings, Isaiah, Jeremiah, Ezekiel, and the Twelve Minor Prophets. The Writings include Psalms, Job, Proverbs, Ruth, Song of Songs, Ecclesiastes, Lamentations, Esther, Daniel, Ezra-Nehemiah, and 1–2 Chronicles.

Bibles produced under Protestant sponsorship like the *Revised Standard Version* or the *New International Version* contain the same material as the Hebrew Bible, but it is divided into thirty-nine books and arranged in quite a different order. A Catholic Bible such as the *New American Bible* or the *Jerusalem Bible* will contain seven more books (Tobit, Judith, 1 Maccabees, 2 Maccabees, Wisdom, Sirach, and Baruch) and somewhat larger editions of Daniel and Esther. Since the additional books in the Catholic canon are interspersed among the historical, wisdom, and prophetic books of the Hebrew Bible, the result is a third order of biblical books.

The book that Christians traditionally call the Old Testament and Jews know as the Hebrew Bible or "Tanak" (from the initial letters of the Hebrew words for Law, Prophets, and Writings) is really a collection of books, something like an anthology or a portable library. Even the individual books within the collection have an anthological character. For example, the book of Exodus is made up of narratives, an ancient song (15:1–18), and various kinds of laws and cultic regulations. The book of Jeremiah blends prose narratives and poetic oracles, and Proverbs consists of blocks of wisdom sayings attributed to Solomon, the sages, Agur, and Lemuel. Within the covers of the Old Testament there is material as early as the twelfth century B.C. (especially hymns) and as late as the second century B.C. (Daniel) or the first century B.C. (Wisdom). Most of the books were composed in Palestine (though Wisdom probably came from Alexandria in Egypt), but they show influences from Egypt, Syria, Persia, Greece, and the other lands of the ancient Near East.

If our browser persists and begins to read parts of the Old Testament, he or she will find more surprises. Some parts of the Bible do not seem very "religious" in the conventional understanding of that term. The Song of Songs appears to be love poetry, and the Psalms are full of talk about vengeance against enemies. The historical books are largely concerned with victories and defeats in battle, and the prophets stand right in the middle of the political affairs of their people. The great ancestors of Israel like Jacob and David perform questionable or even reprehensible actions. The browser's understanding of religion may begin to undergo some necessary adjustments at this point.

What holds together this collection of many writings from over a thousand years of time and from various theological perspectives? It is the conviction that the Bible is the record of God's dealings with his chosen people. God relates to his people in story and song, in proverb and prophecy, in vision and law. God is involved in every aspect of his people's life—in its loves and hates, triumphs and defeats, history and imaginings. God remains faithful to his people in its rebellions, its exiles, and its sufferings. Since it tells the story of God's relationship with his people, the Old Testament promotes a historical and communal religious stance. Christian faith sees in Jesus of Nazareth the culmination of God's relationship to his people and the means by which those not born Jewish may become part of God's people. See my *God's People in Christ: New Testament Perspectives on the Church and Judaism* (Philadelphia: Fortress, 1980).

The documents that make up the Old Testament are pieces of literature, and our understanding and appreciation of them grows when we study them with the basic techniques of literary analysis. These techniques are not very complicated. They demand only that we look seriously at a text and ask ourselves some simple questions. In the effort to answer these questions we begin to penetrate beneath the surface and allow ourselves to be drawn into the dynamic of the text. The Old Testament is never abstract and seldom relies on theological theses or propositions to communicate its religious message. Because the Bible is the record of God's dealings with his people, it communicates in literary forms that touch all the aspects of human life—stories, laws, poems, proverbs, and so forth. The basic techniques of literary analysis are necessary for understanding the Old Testament message.

B.   Literary Analysis

What are the basic concerns of literary analysis? What questions does one ask of a text in order to grasp it more surely and to let oneself be grasped by it? The first concern of literary analysis is the words and images of the text, the materials from which any piece of literature is constructed. Most of the Old Testament is written in ancient Hebrew. Aramaic* passages occur in a few places (Ezra 4:8–6:18; 7:12–26; Dan 2:4–7:28; Jer 10:11; and Gen 31:47). The additional material in the Roman Catholic canon is based on Greek texts, though some of those books were surely composed in Hebrew (e.g., Sirach). Hebrew and Aramaic are closely related Semitic languages, and even the Greek books of the Old Testament were strongly influenced by Semitic patterns of thought and expression. The words and images of the Old Testament reflect the life of a particular people in the ancient Near East. If we are to understand the record of God's dealings with this people, we need first of all to understand the words and images in which that record is expressed.

During the past hundred years or so, the task of analyzing the words and images has been greatly facilitated by the discovery of ancient texts from the Near East. Some of the texts were written in Hebrew, and many more of them are in related Semitic languages like Ugaritic, Akkadian, Aramaic, and now Eblaite. These firsthand witnesses to antiquity frequently shed a penetrating light on the meaning of words in the Old Testament, and sometimes they even make matters more complicated than scholars had previously imagined. Texts in non-Semitic languages like Su-

---

* (Aramaic was a widely-used language in the Middle East, especially from about 700 B.C. onwards. It was an official language in the Persian empire and in later Old Testament times was the language spoken by at least a good portion of the Jews.)

merian, Hittite, and Egyptian can illuminate the meaning of foreign words in the Hebrew texts of the Bible and, most importantly, give valuable information about the customs and social realities that prevailed in the ancient Near East. The point is that words and images in the literature of the Old Testament must be read first and foremost on their own historical terms, and those terms are the languages and customs of a people that lived in the ancient Near East more than two thousand years ago.

The second concern in the literary analysis of the Old Testament is the characters and the movement of the text. Who says or does what to whom? What happens? How have things changed when the text is finished? In some texts there is very little movement. The poetry and proverbs of the Old Testament luxuriate in parallelisms in which the same point is made twice. For example, Psalm 32:1 pronounces blessed one "whose transgression is forgiven, whose sin is covered." In a largely oral culture where traditions were memorized and recited, this device of parallelism was necessary to make sure that the hearers understood the one point. The modern reader who assumes that two points are necessarily being made by the two statements or that there is some gradation between forgiving transgressions and covering sins, fails to take the text on its own terms. On the other hand, the stories of the book of Genesis or the accounts about King David's court show a great deal of movement. In analyzing them we need to focus on the various characters and their relations with one another: Who are the main characters or the focus of attention? How do others relate to them? In what situation were these characters at the beginning of the story, and where do they find themselves at the end?

A third and related concern of literary analysis is the form of the text. How the author has chosen to communicate is intimately related to what is communicated. Wisdom derived from long experience is best presented in a proverb. Direction for a people in crisis is properly cast in a prophetic oracle. Cultic regulations are customarily stated as directives, and laws specify the case and the punishment. The exploits of kings and warriors take the form of a story. The attentive reader, after trying to understand the words and images in the text and to follow the logical flow, will then stand back and ask: What kind of text is this? The twentieth century has it stock of literary forms—the novel, the editorial, the question-and-answer, the free-verse poem, and so on. The people who produced the Scriptures and their neighbors had their own favorite modes of literary communication. To ignore this fact is to guarantee that the Old Testament texts will be misunderstood.

The final concern of literary analysis is the message of the text. The present volume has been written as the introduction to a series of commentaries entitled the *Old Testament Message*. The use of the term "message" may mislead people into thinking that the ultimate goal of biblical study is the theological proposition (e.g., "God is faithful"). It may seem that the analysis of the text's language, movement, and literary form are useful only to isolate the abstract message expressed in general terms. Not so! If the Bible teaches us anything about God's dealings with his people, it is that this relationship touches all aspects of human existence. The "message" of a biblical text is so closely connected with the words and form in which it is expressed that the very medium of communication provides much of the message. Literary form and theological content are intimately related; the former is not simply the means to arrive at the latter.

With these cautions about the "message" in mind, the question of significance remains necessary and valid. The reflective reader wants to know what this text says about

God and human existence, what implications it may have today for the life of individuals or communities, and what transfer value it can have. There are people who are satisfied to study the Old Testament simply as an important document for understanding ancient Near Eastern history and culture. They are content to defer the question of religious truth or have already come to a negative decision about it. But most readers of the Bible come to it as a source of religious insight. Although they often ask the question about the message of the text and its application far too early in the process of interpretation, their basic instinct of asking religious questions of religious literature is sound.

C.   Examples of Literary Criticism

1.   *Genesis 22:1–19.*   The story of God's command to Abraham to sacrifice his only son Isaac has fascinated biblical interpreters for thousands of years. It is highly dramatic and even chilling, and thus it furnishes a good example of what the basic concerns of literary criticism (words and images, characters and movement, form, and message) can bring forth from a biblical passage.

> ¹After these things God tested Abraham, and said to him, "Abraham!" And he said, "Here am I." ²He said, "Take your son, your only son Isaac, whom you love, and go to the land of Moriah, and offer him there as a burnt offering upon one of the mountains of which I shall tell you." ³So Abraham rose early in the morning, saddled his ass, and took two of his young men with him, and his son Isaac; and he cut the wood for the burnt offering, and arose and went to the place of which God had told him. ⁴On the third day Abraham lifted up his eyes and saw the place afar off. ⁵Then Abraham said to his young men,

"Stay here with the ass; I and the lad will go yonder and worship, and come again to you." ⁶And Abraham took the wood of the burnt offering, and laid it on Isaac his son; and he took in his hand the fire and the knife. So they went both of them together. ⁷And Isaac said to his father Abraham, "My father!" And he said, "Here am I, my son." He said, "Behold, the fire and the wood; but where is the lamb for a burnt offering?" ⁸Abraham said, "God will provide himself the lamb for a burnt offering, my son." So they went both of them together.

⁹When they came to the place of which God had told him, Abraham built an altar there, and laid the wood in order, and bound Isaac his son, and laid him on the altar, upon the wood. ¹⁰Then Abraham put forth his hand, and took the knife to slay his son. ¹¹But the angel of the Lord called to him from heaven, and said, "Abraham, Abraham!" And he said, "Here am I." ¹²He said, "Do not lay your hand on the lad or do anything to him; for now I know that you fear God, seeing you have not withheld your son, your only son, from me." ¹³And Abraham lifted up his eyes and looked, and behold, behind him was a ram, caught in a thicket by his horns; and Abraham went and took the ram, and offered it up as a burnt offering instead of his son. ¹⁴So Abraham called the name of that place The Lord will provide; as it is said to this day, "On the mount of the Lord it shall be provided."

¹⁵And the angel of the Lord called to Abraham a second time from heaven, ¹⁶and said, "By myself I have sworn, says the Lord, because you have done this, and have not withheld your son, your only son, ¹⁷I will indeed bless you, and I will multiply your descendants as the stars of heaven and as the sand which is on the seashore. And your descendants shall possess the gate of their enemies, ¹⁸and by your descendants shall all the nations of the earth bless themselves, because you have obeyed my voice." ¹⁹So Abraham returned to his young men, and they arose and went together to Beer-sheba; and Abraham dwelt at Beer-sheba.

The words and images in the passage offer little difficulty. At the very beginning (v. 1) the narrator calls the story a "test," for the account concerns God's command to Abraham to kill the son through whom the only hope of his becoming a great nation (see Gen 12:1–3; 15:1–6; 17:1–18:33; 21:1–34) could be fulfilled. In v. 2 and elsewhere we hear that Isaac is to be made a "burnt offering"—a sacrifice consecrated to God and consumed totally in the fire. Although child sacrifice was practiced in some Near Eastern cultures, the Jewish religious tradition looked upon it with horror and used animal or cereal offerings as sacrifices. In v. 12 Abraham is praised as one who "fears God." In the Old Testament fear of God is not an abject cowering, but rather a realistic understanding of one's relation to God. Fear of God involves faith, respect, and love. The place names in v. 2 ("Moriah") and v. 14 ("The Lord will provide") reflect a play on the Hebrew word "see." Possessing the gate of one's enemies (v. 17) means to have gained control over their cities.

The considerations raised by the movement of this text help to unlock its riches. The story is told by a narrator. He tells us right at the start that this is a test and goes on to unfold before us the tale of Abraham and Isaac. God tells Abraham to offer Isaac. Abraham sets out on a three-day journey with Isaac and two servants. When the place of sacrifice is reached, the servants are dismissed. Isaac wonders aloud about where the lamb might be, and then Abraham prepares his own son for sacrifice.

The whole first part of the story (vv. 1–10) builds up to the moment of crisis: "Then Abraham put forth his hand and took the knife to slay his son." It is a model of effective story telling in that great human emotions are touched in an indirect way. The narrator does not explain to us what Abraham or Isaac felt, but the very way in which the story is told communicates their dread and confusion. The story is unfolded step-by-step, from the divine command through the journey to the place of sacrifice to the moment when Abraham actually draws the knife to kill his only son. This indirect or "cool" approach has the paradoxical effect of drawing the reader more deeply into the emotional experiences of the characters. We share in Abraham's dilemma: God, who promised Abraham descendants through Isaac, now demands that Isaac be sacrificed. We share in the "fear and trembling" of Abraham as he is about to slay his beloved son. We share in Isaac's bewilderment.

The second part of the story (vv. 11–19) resolves the suspense so artistically built up in the first part. A messenger from God intervenes just in the nick of time and tells Abraham not to sacrifice Isaac (vv. 11-12). Since Abraham did not withhold his only son, his faith has been proven. Instead of Isaac, a ram is provided for the sacrifice (vv. 13–14). The second intervention by the messenger reaffirms the blessing of Abraham and his descendants (vv. 15–19).

The form of the text is clear. It is a story. It is told by a narrator who presumably knew the outcome from the start. The narrator built the suspense slowly up to the crisis point in v. 10 and made us participate in Abraham's fear and trembling. He showed us something of Isaac's confusion with the ironic question in v. 7: "But where is the lamb for a burnt offering?" Having skillfully created the atmosphere of suspense and even terror, the narrator then dissolved it in the two angelic interventions in the second part. We come away not only relieved but also convinced of the greatness of Abraham's fidelity toward God.

The message of the text is not easy to reduce to a phrase or a sentence. Nor should it be! The narrative in Gen 22:1–19 brings together the great biblical themes of divine promise, faith, obedience, and testing. It raises the moral dilemma about doing apparent evil in response to a command from

God. It touches on the profound human experience of fear and of facing up to the impending loss of a loved one. At one point in its history the story may even have been used as a help in forbidding the sacrifice of first-born children at cultic centers. The idea would have been that the God of Abraham did not accept this kind of offering. All these dimensions constitute the message of the story and suggest the directions in which we are to be led by it. To reduce the account to a theological proposition stated in abstract language is to ignore the artistic power that has made the story of God's command to Abraham to sacrifice Isaac in Gen 22:1-19 one of the great achievements of literary skill and human sensitivity.

    2. *Isaiah 40:1-11.* The capture of Jerusalem and the destruction of the temple in 587 B.C. marked the end of kingship in Judah after many centuries of relative political autonomy. Nevertheless, the exiles in Babylon kept alive the Jewish religious traditions and the hopes that they would once more be a people with a land and a law. An important step toward realizing those hopes came with the rise of the Persian empire and the policy of its King Cyrus, who allowed subject peoples a great deal of cultural autonomy. This policy gave the Jews exiled in Babylon the permission to return to Jerusalem and resume the worship of God in his holy place. This is the historical situation presupposed in Isaiah 40-55, the chapters customarily called Second Isaiah. No passage better captures the intense enthusiasm that greeted Cyrus' permission in 538 B.C. than the prologue of those chapters (Isa 40:1-11).

> [1]Comfort, comfort my people, says your God. [2]Speak tenderly to Jerusalem, and cry to her that her warfare is ended, that her iniquity is pardoned, that she has received from the Lord's hand double for all her sins. [3]A voice cries: "In the wilderness prepare the way of the Lord,

make straight in the desert a highway for our God. ⁴Every valley shall be lifted up, and every mountain and hill be made low; the uneven ground shall become level, and the rough places a plain. ⁵And the glory of the Lord shall be revealed, and all flesh shall see it together, for the mouth of the Lord has spoken." ⁶A voice says, "Cry!" And I said, "What shall I cry?" All flesh is grass, and all its beauty is like the flower of the field. ⁷The grass withers, the flower fades, when the breath of the Lord blows upon it; surely the people is grass. ⁸The grass withers, the flower fades; but the word of our God will stand for ever. ⁹Get you up to a high mountain, O Zion, herald of good tidings; lift up your voice with strength, O Jerusalem, herald of good tidings, lift it up, fear not; say to the cities of Judah, "Behold your God!" ¹⁰Behold, the Lord God comes with might, and his arm rules for him; behold, his reward is with him, and his recompense before him. ¹¹He will feed his flock like a shepherd, he will gather the lambs in his arms, he will carry them in his bosom, and gently lead those that are with young.

The best approach to this text is to begin with the characters and movement. First in vv. 1–2 God gives several orders ("comfort...speak...cry"). The Hebrew words are clearly plural verbs in the imperative, and it appears that we are to imagine God presiding at an assembly of angelic beings in the heavenly council or court. God is informing other supernatural or angelic beings that Israel's time of punishment is over. Then in vv. 3–5 an anonymous herald ("a voice cries") proclaims to the other members of the assembly that the Lord will soon return his people from Babylon to the place of his glory. In the next movement (vv. 6–8) another anonymous herald ("a voice") addresses the prophet ("and I said") and assures him of the power of God's word and tells him to proclaim the good news of God's leading his people back to their homeland. The prophet seems to have been present at the heavenly council, and his task is to serve as the messenger of God to his people. At the end of the passage (vv. 9-11) the prophet is poetically transformed into the city of Jerusalem ("O Zion, herald of good tidings...O Jerusalem, herald of good tidings").

The words and images of the passage are so rich that only two points—the language used with reference to God and the exodus language in vv. 3-5—can be treated here. How is God described? The traditional titles God and Lord (Yahweh) are used. God presides at a meeting of heavenly beings (vv. 1-2), an image used in all sorts of Mesopotamian religious texts. God is presented as making his way in the wilderness, and before him the path is smoothed (vv. 3-5). His word is not merely beautiful like grass and flowers but also lasting in contrast to strictly human things (vv. 6-8). Finally, God is a warrior (v. 10) and a shepherd (v. 11). Thus the passage combines many titles and images of God and moves rapidly from one to another.

The references to the Lord's way in the wilderness (vv. 3-5) are crucial, for they represent the initial effort in Second Isaiah at interpreting the return from exile in light of the escape from Egypt under the leadership of Moses. The exodus from Egypt furnished the pattern or type for Israel's hopes in the sixth century B.C., and the exodus-motif runs like a thread through the whole of Second Isaiah (see Isa 41:17-20; 42:14-16; 43:1-3, 14-21; 48:20-21; 49:8-12; 51:9-10; 52:11-12; 55:12-13). In other words, the most appropriate words and images that the prophet could find to describe the hopes connected with the return from exile was the language complex previously used to describe the liberation that first made Israel into a people. The return to Jerusalem is a new exodus!

If parallelism is the basic device of Hebrew poetry, then Isa 40:1-11 surely qualifies as a poem. From beginning to end the ideas are repeated in varying forms: "Comfort... speak tenderly...he will carry...and gently lead." The structure of the poem is determined to a large extent by the characters who engage in the dialogue: God and the council (vv. 1–2), the anonymous herald (vv. 3–5), the herald and the prophet (vv. 6–8), and the prophet as Jerusalem (vv. 9–11). The many images, the emotional tone, and the visionary atmosphere all mark the passage as a poem.

The message is joy that Israel's exile is over and hope that a new beginning, comparable to the exodus from Egypt, is about to take place in Jerusalem. Once more the richness of the experience of renewal is captured in the literary form in which the message is expressed. The parallelisms, the dialogues, the rapid shifts in imagery, and the mood of mystery invite the reader to share in the joy that the period of suffering is over and in the hope that the new age will bring freedom and right relationship with God. These deeply human and religious feelings could never have been adequately expressed in abstract language or theological propositions.

Summary.   The Old Testament is a varied collection of writings held together by the conviction that it is the record of God's dealings with his chosen people. Our understanding of these pieces of literature grows when we approach them with the questions involved in basic literary criticism. The concerns of literary criticism are the words and images in the text, the characters and movements, the literary form, and the message.

Bibliography: Literary Criticism

L. Alonso Schökel, *The Inspired Word: Scripture in the Light of Language and Literature* (New York: Herder & Herder, 1965).

R. Alter, *The Art of Biblical Narrative* (New York: Basic Books, 1981); *The Art of Biblical Poetry* (1985).

R. Alter and F. Kermode (eds.), *The Literary Guide to the Bible* (Cambridge, MA: Harvard University Press, 1987).

B.W. Anderson, *Understanding the Old Testament* (4th ed.; Englewood Cliffs, NJ: Prentice-Hall, 1986).

J. Barton, *Reading the Old Testament: Method in Biblical Study* (Philadelphia: Westminster, 1984).

L. Boadt, *Reading the Old Testament. An Introduction* (New York—Mahwah, NJ: Paulist, 1984).

B.S. Childs, *Introduction to the Old Testament as Scripture* (Philadelphia: Fortress, 1979).

N. Frye, *The Great Code. The Bible and Literature* (New York—London: Harcourt Brace Jovanovich, 1982).

O. Eissfeldt, *The Old Testament: An Introduction* (Oxford: Blackwell, 1965).

N. Habel, *Literary Criticism of the Old Testament* (Philadelphia: Fortress, 1971).

J.H. Hayes, *An Introduction to Old Testament Study* (Nashville: Abingdon, 1979).

D.A. Knight and G.M. Tucker (eds.), *The Hebrew Bible and Its Modern Interpreters* (Philadelphia: Fortress, 1985).

D. Robertson, *The Old Testament and the Literary Critic* (Philadelphia: Fortress, 1971).

2. HISTORICAL CRITICISM

A. Israel's History

WHAT REALLY HAPPENED? That is the question that occupies the historical critic of the Old Testament. The question is often hard to answer, since the biblical writers did not set out to write "objective history" according to nineteenth and twentieth-century A.D. standards. Even in the so-called historical books of the Old Testament such as 1–2 Kings or Ezra, the writers were mainly concerned to promote a definite religious stance and judged the characters in the traditional stories according to their conformity to the religious stance. For example, the famous Ahab, who was king in Israel in the ninth century B.C., was roundly criticized by the Deuteronomic historian but might well be praised by moderns for his political and military achievements. In the more picturesque accounts of Genesis and Exodus, it can be even harder to sort out historical fact from theological interpretation.

Nothing in the Old Testament gives us anything like a videotape record of the events. We are always dealing with interpreted events. This chapter will first provide a sketch

of Israel's history from the patriarchs to Alexander the
Great's conquest of Palestine and then will focus on the
problems involved in trying to say what happened in the
exodus from Egypt.

The stories about the great ancestors of Israel—the
patriarchs Abraham, Isaac, and Jacob—reflect Near
Eastern life in the first half of the second millenium B.C.
(2000-1600 B.C.). The patriarchs appear to have been historical persons, and the accounts about them contain
names, legal customs, and other information that are par-
alleled in extrabiblical documents contemporaneous with
their careers. But the narratives about the patriarchs in
Genesis 12-50 are generally not the kind of solid factual
writing from which modern historians can develop a coher-
ent history of Israel's beginnings.

The real history of Israel begins in the early thirteenth
century B.C. with the people's escape from Egypt under
the leadership of Moses. Although the stories about Moses
in the books of Exodus and Numbers breathe the same atmosphere as those about the patriarchs in Genesis, it is
hard to explain the subsequent course of Israel's history
and religion without such a dominant figure as Moses and
without such an event as the exodus. After the escape from
Egypt the people formed in the area to the south of Canaan
and joined in a covenant relationship with the God Yahweh. The concept of covenant and the divine name Yahweh probably have continuity with the patriarchal religion.
What was new about the Mosaic religion was the emphasis
on the escape from Egypt as the great act of God on behalf
of his people.

The entrance into the land of Canaan took place in the
late thirteenth century, but it is difficult to be sure about
the extent of this conquest. The archaeological evidence is
ambiguous, with some excavations yielding evidence of a
military conquest and others (e.g., at Jericho) tilting

towards a symbolic interpretation of the biblical account. At any rate, the picture of a single force under the leadership of Joshua systematically conquering all the Canaanites is not likely and indeed is contradicted by the book of Judges. Modern historians of the conquest take into account the possibility of more than one invading force and the likelihood that the invaders were joined by adherents of the old patriarchal faith who were already living in Palestine.

Israel did not gain complete control of the land until the time of King David. The period between the invasion of the land of Canaan around 1200 B.C. and the anointing of Saul around 1020 B.C. is called the time of the judges. Not only did many Canaanite cities remain unconquered, but also there were invasions by the Philistines, Moabites, and Midianites in the twelfth century and by the Ammonites in the eleventh century. The leaders of the Israelite resistance to these invasions were called judges—charismatic leaders who emerged at various times and in various places to rally as many tribes in the Israelite confederation as would join in the battle. In the twelfth century the Israelite league defeated a coalition of Canaanite kings (see Judges 5), but in the eleventh century the Philistines united under the king of Gath and gained the upper hand. The ark of the covenant from Israel's central shrine at Shiloh was captured around 1050 B.C. Samuel, the last of the judges, was forced to change the structure of Israel from covenant league to a monarchy under King Saul in order to meet the Philistine threat more effectively.

The period of Saul (1020–1000), David (1000–961), and Solomon (961–922) was marked by military and political success. Saul had his capital at Gibeah and won some victories against the Philistines before his death in the battle of Gilboa. David became king in Judah on Saul's death and soon also gained control over the northern tribes. By conquering Jerusalem and making it the capital for all Israel, David freed himself from intertribal disputes. To this "neutral" city he brought the ark of the covenant and set up a central shrine, thus establishing continuity with the people's past while carrying out a dramatic religious and political innovation. The sagas of the patriarchs, the exodus, and the judges were probably collected into the so-called Yahwist epic at this time. David defeated the Philistines and made a treaty with Hiram the king of Tyre.

Solomon (961–922) was even more innovative and ambitious than his father David had been. He directed the building of a temple similar in plan and decoration to the Canaanite temples of his time, except that the ark of the covenant had the central place. He reorganized the system of gathering taxes and expanded his army. Building operations were carried out not only in Jerusalem but also in other cities. Treaties and diplomatic marriages made his kingdom secure and left him free to arrange various commercial ventures. Solomon was a truly international figure, and during his reign Israel became "like the nations" in the fullest sense of the phrase. But after Solomon's death in 922 B.C. and the accession of his son Rehoboam, a rebellion occurred that split Israel into two kingdoms. Rehoboam remained as king in Judah (the south), and Jeroboam I became king in Israel (the north).

The two hundred years in the history of the northern kingdom of Israel (922-722 B.C.) began with Jeroboam's setting up of Bethel as a cultic center in competition with Jerusalem. There was a rapid succession of dynasties from Baasha to Omri to Jehu, accompanied by frequent assassinations and rebellions. Omri (876–869) moved the capital from Tirzah to Samaria, and his son Ahab was bitterly opposed by Elijah the prophet. The kingdom of Israel came to an abrupt end in 722 B.C. with the capture of Samaria by the Assyrians.

The three-hundred and thirty-five years of Judah's history (922–587 B.C.) were marked by a more orderly succession of rulers, but as was the case in the north the kings were often occupied in dangerous military ventures and alliances with foreign powers. Among the most famous kings of Judah were Uzziah (783-742), Ahaz (734-715), Hezekiah (715–687), and Josiah (640–609). The latter drove out foreign cults from Jerusalem and launched a political-religious reform on the basis of the discovery of an old law book, probably the nucleus of the present book of Deuteronomy. Josiah's successors shifted allegiances between the Babylonians and Egyptians, and in 587 B.C. Nebuchadnezzar captured the city of Jerusalem and destroyed the temple. The wealthy and powerful citizens of Judah were taken to Babylon in a series of three deportations (597, 587, 582).

The time of captivity in Babylon saw the collection and editing of the so-called Deuteronomic history (Deuteronomy, Joshua, Judges, 1-2 Samuel, and 1-2 Kings), the Priestly edition of the Pentateuch, and the prophecies of Ezekiel and Second Isaiah. When Babylon fell to the Persian king Cyrus in 539 B.C., many Jews were allowed to return to Jerusalem and from 520 B.C. work on the restoration of the Jerusalem temple was carried out under the urging of the prophet Haggai. In 445 B.C. Nehemiah came as governor to Jerusalem and rebuilt the walls of the city, and in 428 B.C. Ezra began his religious and legal reforms. Alexander the Great conquered Palestine in 332 B.C. For a sketch of Jewish history from Alexander to A.D. 100, see my *Interpreting the New Testament*, pp. 109–113.

B. Escape from Egypt

In the sketch of Israel's history I emphasized the decisive importance of Israel's escape from Egypt in the thirteenth century B.C. under the leadership of Moses. That Moses was a historical figure and led forth from Egypt a sizable group of people can scarcely be doubted. But what was the nature of that event?

The Old Testament contains several versions of the exodus, and historical criticism aims to sift through these accounts in an effort at answering the question: What really happened? As we will see, it is easier to say *that* the exodus happened than it is to determine *what* precisely took place. The major problem is that the biblical writers did not share our modern preoccupation with objective descriptions of past events. The significance of the event as a sign of God's presence to his people was far more important than the precise details.

The following discussion of the three accounts about the exodus from Egypt in Exodus 14–15 presupposes some of the material treated on pp. 86–87 in the chapter on source criticism and redaction criticism. It is based on the widespread critical acceptance of the hypothesis that in the present form of the book of Exodus it is possible to discern the remnants of three documents: Priestly (P), Yahwist (J), and Elohist (E). As we will see, the poem presented in Exodus 15 represents an even earlier stage of literary tradition. The division of sources adopted here is the conventional one found in most modern commentaries on Exodus and in critical introductions to the Old Testament. The point of the discussion here is not to defend the source analysis, but rather to illustrate how one event can be described in three different ways in the course of two chapters of the Bible.

The story of Israel's escape from Egypt in Exodus 14:1–31 has long been recognized as a composite of at least two accounts. When the material representing typically Priestly vocabulary and concerns is separated out, there emerges a narrative in which the Lord gives three commands (vv. 1–4,

15-18, 26) and the commands are carried out (vv. 8-9; 21a, 21c, 22-23; 27a, 28-29).

[1]Then the Lord said to Moses, [2]"Tell the people of Israel to turn back and encamp in front of Pihahiroth, between Migdol and the sea, in front of Baalzephon; you shall encamp over against it, by the sea. [3]For Pharaoh will say of the people of Israel, 'They are entangled in the land; the wilderness has shut them in.' [4]And I will harden Pharaoh's heart, and he will pursue them and I will get glory over Pharaoh and all his host; and the Egyptians shall know that I am the Lord." And they did so.

[8]And the Lord hardened the heart of Pharaoh king of Egypt and he pursued the people of Israel as they went forth defiantly. [9]The Egyptians pursued them, all Pharaoh's horses and chariots and his horsemen and his army, and overtook them encamped at the sea, by Pihahiroth, in front of Baalzephon.

[15]The Lord said to Moses, "Why do you cry to me? Tell the people of Israel to go forward. [16]Lift up your rod, and stretch out your hand over the sea and divide it, that the people of Israel may go on dry ground through the sea. [17]And I will harden the hearts of the Egyptians so that they shall go in after them, and I will get glory over Pharaoh and all his host, his chariots, and his horsemen. [18]And the Egyptians shall know that I am the Lord, when I have gotten glory over Pharaoh, his chariots, and his horsemen."

[21]Then Moses stretched out his hand over the sea; and the waters were divided. [22]And the people of Israel went into the midst of the sea on dry ground, the waters being a wall to them on their right hand and on their left. [23]The Egyptians pursued, and went in after them into the midst of the sea, all Pharaoh's horses, his chariots, and his horsemen.

[26]Then the Lord said to Moses, "Stretch out your hand over the sea, that the water may come back upon the

Egyptians, upon their chariots, and upon their horsemen." [27]So Moses stretched forth his hand over the sea, and the sea returned to its wonted flow when the morning appeared. [28]The waters returned and covered the chariots and the horsemen and all the host of Pharaoh that had followed them into the sea; not so much as one of them remained. [29]But the people of Israel walked on dry ground through the sea, the waters being a wall to them on their right hand and on their left.

According to this account the Lord instructed Moses to have the people camp "by the sea" and then inspired the king of Egypt to pursue them. Then the Lord told Moses to divide the sea by lifting up his rod. When the sea was divided, Israel passed over between two walls of water. Finally Moses is commanded to stretch out his hand over the sea and bring back the waters over the Egyptians. This is the spectacular account of the exodus from Egypt brought to the movie screen in Cecil B. DeMille's "The Ten Commandments."

A second account of the escape from Egypt has been combined with the Priestly story. It appears to have been the Yahwist (J) account supplemented by Elohist (E) touches. In other words, the second account probably comes from the epic source put together after 722 B.C. on the basis of J and E. The Elohist material is said to be found in vv. 5a, 7, 19a, 25a. The second account taken as a whole embraces vv. 5-7, 10-14, 19-20, 21b, 24-25, 27b, 30-31. When put together the JE account looks like this:

[5]When the king of Egypt was told that the people had fled, the mind of Pharaoh and his servants was changed toward the people, and they said, "What is this we have done, that we have let Israel go from serving us?" [6]So he made ready his chariot and took his army with him, [7]and took six hundred picked chariots and all the other chariots of Egypt with officers over all of them.

[10]When Pharaoh drew near, the people of Israel lifted up their eyes, and behold, the Egyptians were marching after them; and they were in great fear. And the people of Israel cried out to the Lord; [11]and they said to Moses, "Is it because there are no graves in Egypt that you have taken us away to die in the wilderness? What have you done to us, in bringing us out of Egypt? [12]Is not this what we said to you in Egypt, 'Let us alone and let us serve the Egyptians'? For it would have been better for us to serve the Egyptians than to die in the wilderness." [13]And Moses said to the people, "Fear not, stand firm, and see the salvation of the Lord, which he will work for you today; for the Egyptians whom you see today, you shall never see again. [14]The Lord will fight for you, and you have only to be still."

[19]Then the angel of God who went before the host of Israel moved and went behind them; and the pillar of cloud moved from before them and stood behind them, [20]coming between the host of Egypt and the host of Israel. And there was the cloud and the darkness; and the night passed without one coming near the other all night.

[21]And the Lord drove the sea back by a strong east wind all night, and made the sea dry land.

[24]And in the morning watch the Lord in the pillar of fire and of cloud looked down upon the host of the Egyptians, and discomfited the host of the Egyptians, [25]clogging their chariot wheels so that they drove heavily; and the Egyptians said, "Let us flee from before Israel; for the Lord fights for them against the Egyptians."

[27]And the Egyptians fled into it, and the Lord routed the Egyptians in the midst of the sea.

[30]Thus the Lord saved Israel that day from the hand of the Egyptians; and Israel saw the Egyptians dead upon the seashore. [31]And Israel saw the great work which the Lord did against the Egyptians, and the people feared the Lord; and they believed in the Lord and in his servant Moses.

According to this story the king of Egypt changed his mind about letting the Israelites go, whereas in the Priestly account God hardened Pharaoh's heart. Here the conversation is between Moses and the people, not between Moses and God. The crossing over is made possible by a strong east wind during the night that dried up the sea (v. 21). The Egyptians are destroyed by getting their chariots caught up in the marshy ground. The event is presented as proof that God has been with Moses all along and will continue to bless his leadership.

Neither the Priestly nor the Yahwist-Elohist account of Israel's liberation from Egypt is the oldest version in the Old Testament. Exodus 15:1-12 contains a poem that celebrates God's victory over the Egyptians. Its language and poetic form mark it as one of the oldest compositions in the Old Testament—from the twelfth or eleventh century B.C.

> [1]Then Moses and the people of Israel sang this song to the Lord, saying, "I will sing to the Lord, for he has triumphed gloriously; the horse and his rider he has thrown into the sea. [2]The Lord is my strength and my song, and he has become my salvation; this is my God, and I will praise him, my father's God, and I will exalt him. [3]The Lord is a man of war; the Lord is his name. [4]Pharaoh's chariots and his host he cast into the sea; and his picked officers are sunk in the Reed Sea. [5]The floods cover them; they went down into the depths like a stone. [6]Thy right hand, O Lord, glorious in power, thy right hand, O Lord, shatters the enemy. [7]In the greatness of thy majesty thou overthrowest thy adversaries; thou sendest forth thy fury, it consumes them like stubble. [8]At the blast of thy nostrils the waters piled up, the floods stood up in a heap; the deeps congealed in the heart of the sea. [9]The enemy said, 'I will pursue, I will overtake, I will divide the spoil, my desire shall have its fill of them. I will draw my sword, my hand shall destroy them.' [10]Thou didst blow

with thy wind, the sea covered them; they sank as lead in the mighty waters. [11]Who is like thee, O Lord, among the gods? Who is like thee, majestic in holiness, terrible in glorious deeds, doing wonders? [12]Thou didst stretch out thy right hand, the earth swallowed them.

The many parallelisms, the meter, the rich imagery, and the emotional tone indicate that this account is a song. It praises God as a warrior who has shown his might in defeating Israel's enemies and delights in contrasting the real power of the Lord with the foolish arrogance of the Egyptians. Thus the oldest account of the exodus is more concerned with the superiority of Yahweh ("Who is like thee, O Lord, among the gods?") than in giving a precise description of the particulars of the event at the Reed Sea. Comparison of Exod 15:1-12 with the Priestly account in chapter 14 suggests that the latter is a prose version of the former. For example, the source of the "Cecil B. DeMille" version of the crossing of the sea found in Exod 14:22 may well be the poetic language of Exod 15:8: "At the blast of thy nostrils the waters piled up, the floods stood up in a heap; the deeps congealed in the heart of the sea."

One event, three accounts. The event—the escape from Egypt—took place in the thirteenth century. The earliest available presentation of it is found in a poem from the twelfth or eleventh century. The earliest prose version (JE) comes from the late eighth century, though that account surely depended on earlier sources. The latest version appears to be a prose presentation on the basis of the poetic account in Exod 15:1-12.

None of these accounts was concerned to any great extent with the details of the exodus event. Their primary concern was the celebration of God's power as a warrior (poetic account), the exodus as a sign of God's presence to his people (JE), and God's ability fo fulfill what he commands (P). Twentieth-century A.D. readers might like to know more of the particulars, but the sources available to us allow us to go only so far. It would be a pity if our modern preoccupation with "facts" led us to ignore the religious insights that the biblical writers wished to impart.

Summary.   Historical criticism tries to determine what really happened by means of the analysis of the relevant sources. The task is often very difficult in the Old Testament, chiefly because the authors of the documents were more interested in pointing out the religious significance of the events than in providing an accurate factual record of the details of these events.

Bibliography: Historical Criticism

Y. Aharoni, *The Land of the Bible: A Historical Geography* (rev. ed.; Philadelphia: Westminster, 1980).

W.F. Albright, *The Biblical Period from Abraham to Ezra* (New York—Evanston: Harper & Row, 1963).

W.F. Albright, *From Stone Age to Christianity* (New York: Doubleday, 1957).

A. Alt, *Essays on Old Testament History and Religion* (Garden City, NY: Anchor, 1968).

D. Baly, *God and History in the Old Testament* (New York: Harper & Row, 1976).

E. Bickerman, *From Ezra to the Last of the Maccabees* (New York: Schocken, 1962).

J. Bright, *Early Israel in Recent History Writing: A Study in Method* (London: SCM, 1956).

J. Bright, *A History of Israel* (3rd ed.; Philadelphia: Westminster, 1981).

F.M. Cross, *Canaanite Myth and Hebrew Epic* (Cambridge, MA: Harvard University Press, 1972).

R. de Vaux, *Ancient Israel: Its Life and Institutions* (New York: McGraw-Hill, 1961).

R. de Vaux, *The Early History of Israel* (Philadelphia: Westminster, 1978).

H.L. Ellison, *From Babylon to Bethlehem* (Atlanta: John Knox, 1976).

N. Gottwald, *The Tribes of Yahweh: A Sociology of the Religion of Liberated Israel 1250-1051 B.C.E.* (Maryknoll, NY: Orbis, 1979).

J.H. Hayes and J.M. Miller (eds.), *Israelite and Judaean History* (Philadelphia: Westminster, 1977).

S. Hermann, *A History of Israel in Old Testament Times* (Philadelphia: Fortress, 1981).

J.M. Miller, *The Old Testament and the Historian* (Philadelphia: Fortress, 1976).

J.M. Miller and J.H. Hayes, *A History of Ancient Israel and Judah* (Philadelphia: Westminster, 1986).

M. Noth, *The History of Israel* (2nd ed.; New York: Harper & Row, 1958).

J.B. Pritchard (ed.), *The Harper Atlas of the Bible* (San Francisco: Harper & Row, 1987).

H. Ringgren, *Israelite Religion* (Philadelphia: Fortress, 1966).

N.M. Sarna, *Exploring Exodus* (New York: Schocken, 1986).

3. ARCHAEOLOGY AND PARALLELS FROM ANTIQUITY

A. Archaeology

DURING THE PAST two hundred years archaeological discoveries in the Near East have illuminated in striking ways the material culture and spiritual atmosphere in which the books of the Old Testament took shape. The text and language of the Old Testament, the history of Israel and of its neighbors, and the culture of the ancient Near East appear much clearer, thanks to the labors and the achievements of the field archaeologists.

There are two basic ways of doing archaeology: surface exploration and excavation. Surface exploration consists of visits to sites with the goal of gathering clues from pottery and other artifacts as to the history and material culture of the area. It is basically a walk in the countryside. But the trained eye of the archaeologist can turn the walk into a very productive experience, for the Near East yields the secrets of its past quite readily to those who are equipped to uncover them.

Excavation is the systematic digging up of a site. In antiquity when a city was destroyed through natural disasters or by the armies of an enemy, it was customary to rebuild on the same site. A succession of reconstructions would naturally turn the site into a hill or mound called a "tell." Excavating a tell means peeling off these layers of occupation until the bottom is reached.

To excavate completely a tell or even one layer would be prohibitively expensive and very time consuming, and so the usual procedure is to dig holes at several promising places on the site. The various levels in the trenches provide samples for mapping out the history of an ancient city. For example, a heavy black line in the cross-section of earth may suggest that the city had been destroyed by fire at one time. A coin bearing a date or a weapon known to have gone out of fashion at a particular time can provide a fixed point that will allow the archaeologist to put other phases in the cross-section into a chronological order. It is, of course, imperative to go slowly and to record every find carefully, if the history of the site is to be worked out. It is a fact that archaeology proceeds by destroying much of its evidence. Unless that evidence is accurately recorded and eventually published, the excavation may well be just an expensive kind of vandalism. Furthermore, archaeology is not a treasure hunt. Treasures may be uncovered in the process. But unless the treasures can be related to specific points in the site's history, their scientific value is considerably lessened.

Pottery serves as an especially useful guide to archaeologists in their efforts at dating the different levels of occupation on a site. In the ancient Near East ceramics were widely used for storing liquids, for dishes, and for other purposes in everyday life. When these vessels were broken, they were discarded. The broken and discarded pottery is important to archaeologists, because it is frequently possible for them to work out the course of development in style and technology of the pottery. Styles come and go; new materials are substituted for old ones. When the sequence of styles and materials is charted out, the archaeologist has a precious means of making sense out of the mute evidence of the tell. A pot made in 800 B.C. is quite different from ones made in 500 B.C. or A.D. 200. By bringing the pot into relation with the other materials found in the area surrounding it, the archaeologist can learn a good deal about the history of a place.

The most important period in Palestinian archaeology for understanding the Old Testament is called the Iron Age. This era takes its name from the appearance of iron weapons and tools in Palestine in the twelfth century B.C. and extends into the sixth century B.C. Some Israelite cities were founded in this era, but many merely followed the already existing Canaanite patterns. The cities were often built on hills (Jerusalem, Gezer, Gibeon, Samaria) or were encircled at least partially by valleys or by brooks (Jerusalem, Lachish) for easy defense against enemy armies. Proximity to supplies of water was also a key factor in the location of the Israelite cities. The population of Palestine in the Iron Age has been estimated at less than one million people, with one-third in Judah (the southern kingdom) and two-thirds in Israel (the northern kingdom).

What kinds of things do archaeologists learn about Palestine during the Iron Age (ca. 1200 to 600 B.C.)? The systematic excavation of various tells yields a good picture of the fortifications employed in the major cities. Even cities built on hills were enclosed by sturdy walls of stone for the defense of their citizens. While at first the walls were constructed so that their inner areas could serve as storage places, later stronger and more solid walls were used to repulse battering-rams and other military devices. The city gates were designed in pincer form with several series of piers, each of which could be shut down in case of attack. Toward the end of the Iron Age many cities in Palestine had gates that demanded indirect access. Visitors had to go into a narrow passage and proceed under the watchful eyes of guards before they could enter the gate area. Sometimes strongholds were built in the highest places as a means of insuring a place for a last-ditch defense of the city.

Besides protecting the city from hostile attacks, the Iron Age builders in Palestine had to secure an adequate supply of water for the inhabitants. Inside the walls deep wells could be dug with little difficulty, and a system of storage tanks or cisterns to catch the rainfall was a common way of meeting the needs of the people. But wells and cisterns within the city walls frequently failed to supply enough water, and so water supplies outside the city were called upon. These outside supplies presented no problem in times of peace. But what would happen during a siege? If an enemy army surrounded a city and prevented the population from going outside to draw water, the besieged city could be conquered easily. Thus in several cities (Jerusalem, Megiddo, Gibeon, Gezer) tunnels were built that began from within the walls of the city and proceeded under the walls to underground supplies of water. These projects allowed access to water even in times of attack.

It is also possible to learn about the materials and the architecture of the buildings within the city walls. In excavations the foundations and the walls of public buildings and private habitations are frequently exposed, and these partial exposures allow archaeologists to fill in the missing pieces and give a good idea of what Iron Age cities were like to live in. Squares, storage places, streets, provisions for sewerage, and stables are among the architectural objects of interest to the archaeologist. Pottery, jewelry, coins, tools, weapons, and textiles shed light on the daily life of those who lived in these cities. The cities were small and crowded, like the fortified cities of medieval Europe, though in Jerusalem the location of the walls was shifted to accommodate the growing population.

Surface exploration and excavation can provide information about the physical context or environment in which the people mentioned in the Bible and those who wrote its books lived and died. But the evidence uncovered by archaeology is partial, for only a relatively few ancient cities have been systematically investigated. Even in those that have been properly excavated, it is only select areas at the site that have been dug. Most archaeological evidence is mute. It needs interpretation by human beings trained in history and literature, experts capable of drawing comparisons with materials found elsewhere, and physical scientists familiar with the techniques and results of geology. Viewed in this broadly humanistic perspective, archaeology is capable of assisting the mute stones to speak.

B. Ancient Texts

Not all archaeological discoveries are totally mute. The advances in modern biblical scholarship during recent years have been made possible to a large extent by the discovery of non-biblical texts in various parts of the Near East. These texts allow us to place the books of the Bible more exactly in their historical setting and to understand what their authors were trying to communicate. Such texts are found written on stone and pottery fragments (inscriptions), baked clay tablets (the Ebla documents), leather scrolls (the Dead Sea scrolls), or sheets of papyrus (documents from Egypt). These documents are often interesting for their own sake and cast a beam of light on cultures and societies that had been long forgotten. In biblical studies

they frequently illuminate difficult terms and help to resolve problems encountered in interpreting obscure passages.

In a book of this scope it is not possible or useful to
catalogue all the written materials discovered in the Near
East. But some examples will illustrate what these newly
discovered texts can contribute to the understanding of
specific biblical texts. In few, if any, cases is it possible to
prove a relationship of direct literary dependence; that is,
that the biblical writer had a copy of the parallel text or
knew it by memory. Our knowledge of the ancient world is
still too fragmentary to allow much more than pointing out
the striking similarities between two bodies of ancient
literature and suggesting a possible historical connection
between them.

1. *Exodus 21:23-25.*   Chapters 19—24 in the book of
Exodus tell of God's covenant with Moses and the people
of Israel on Mount Sinai. After the Ten Commandments
(Exod 20:2-17), chap. 21 begins a series of "ordinances,"
in which a case is stated ("if such and such happens") and
a resolution or a punishment ("then...") is specified. In
the midst of one of these ordinances, a famous principle is
brought forth in Exod 21:23-25: "If any harm follows,
then you shall give life for life, eye for eye, tooth for tooth,
hand for hand, foot for foot, burn for burn, wound for
wound, stripe for stripe." This law of retaliation is
sometimes cited as proof of cruelty in the Old Testament,
but in fact the law sought to keep vengeance within bounds
and to forestall an endless, escalating cycle of violence.

Several ordinances in the Code of Hammurabi reflect
the same legal principle as Exod 21:23-25 does. Hammurabi was a Babylonian king who reigned in the late eighteenth and early seventeenth centuries B.C. He seems to
have promulgated a legal code during his reign. A copy of
the code inscribed on a diorite pillar was discovered in the
early nineteenth century A.D. at the ancient Elamite capital

of Susa by French archaeologists and brought to Paris. The laws are presented according to the form of cases, as in Exod 21:23-25: "If a free man has knocked out a tooth of a free man of his own rank, they shall knock out his tooth (200)." The case is given, and the punishment is spelled out. The law of retaliation within specified limits is operative here and elsewhere in the code. Similar cases concern destroying the eye of another (196) or the bone of another (197), and the punishments are the destroying of the offender's eye and the breaking of his bone.

There is no good reason to assume that the final author of Exodus knew the code of Hammurabi, though it is not impossible. But the two texts are separated by several centuries, many miles, and different languages. The parallel, however, does show that the rule of proportionality or of retaliation within limits was an important legal principle in antiquity and that it sought to restrain cruelty rather than sanction it. The parallel also introduces us to a typical formula for stating laws in the ancient Near East: "If...then..."

2. *Psalms.* In 1929 at Ras Shamra on the north Syrian coast, the remains of a city destroyed around 1200 B.C. came to light. The city was identified as Ugarit, one of the major Canaanite city-states of the second millennium B.C. Among the many texts in various languages that were found there were clay tablets from the library of the chief priest of the god Baal. They contained stories of the gods and human beings, and some of them may have been used in temple rituals.

The sacred texts from Ugarit have proved especially illuminating for the Old Testament book of Psalms. These two bodies of literature share many phrases and use similar devices such as repetition, parallels, and numerical formulas. Though their theologies are quite different (polytheism versus monotheism), the titles for God and the patterns of thought are common to the two collections. The fact that the Ugaritic texts were found beside the temple of Baal and the Psalms were surely used for worship in the Jerusalem temple indicates that the two bodies of literature functioned in similar settings.

The quotation of a few lines from the Ugaritic Baal epic will illustrate the parallels between it and some passages from the book of Psalms.

> "Let me tell you, Prince Baal,
>   let me repeat, Rider on the Clouds;
> Behold, your enemy, Baal,
>   behold, you will kill your enemy,
>   behold, you will annihilate your foes.
> You will take your eternal kingship,
>   your dominion forever and ever."

The passage is repetitive and is structured according to double and triple parallelisms. Though there are seven lines, there are only three ideas: permission to speak, Baal's destroying the enemy, and Baal's eternal rule.

Besides the formal similarities, there are striking parallels of content between this passage from the Ugaritic Baal epic and the Psalms. Psalm 68 describes Israel's God as the one "who rides upon the clouds" (v. 4) and "who rides in the heavens" (v. 33), in much the same way as Baal is called "Rider on the Clouds." The part about the destruction of Baal's enemies sounds very much like Psalm 92:9:

> "For lo, thy enemies, O Lord,
>   for lo, thy enemies shall perish;
>   all evil doers shall be scattered."

In both texts there are three phrases, and the content is practically the same. Another striking parallel in content is supplied by the final part of the Baal passage and Psalm 145:13:

"Thy kingdom is an everlasting kingdom,
and thy dominion endures throughout all
generations."

These parallels in content suggest that we are dealing with stock-phrases having wide currency in the ancient Near East. They indicate that the Old Testament book of Psalms should not be simply called the hymn book of the Second Temple. Rather, the language and the content of the Psalms go far back into the religious history of the ancient Near East.

Summary.   Surface explorations and excavations during recent years have provided important information about the environment in which the people of the Old Testament lived. Ancient documents like the Code of Hammurabi and the Ugaritic Baal epic supply illuminating parallels to biblical passages. They suggest that some of the Old Testament traditions take us very far back into ancient Near Eastern history and culture.

Bibliography: Archaeology

Y. Aharoni, *The Archaeology of the Land of Israel* (Philadelphia: Westminster, 1982).

W.F. Albright, *The Archaeology of Palestine* (rev. ed.; Baltimore: Penguin, 1961).

N. Avigad, *Discovering Jerusalem* (Nashville: Nelson, 1983).

M. Avi-Yonah and E. Stern (eds.), *Encyclopedia of Archaeological Excavations in the Holy Land* (4 vols.; Englewood Cliffs, NJ: Prentice-Hall, 1975-78).

W. Beyerlin (ed.), *Near Eastern Religious Texts Relating to the Old Testament* (Philadelphia: Westminster, 1978).

G. Cornfeld, *Archaeology of the Bible Book by Book* (New York: Harper & Row, 1976).

W. G. Dever and H.D. Lance (eds.), *A Manual of Field Excavation: Handbook for Field Archaeologists* (Cincinnati—New York—Los Angeles—Jerusalem: Hebrew Union College—Jewish Institute of Religion, 1978).

D.N. Freedman and J.C. Greenfield (eds.), *New Directions in Biblical Archaeology* (Garden City, NY: Doubleday, 1969).

L. Hoppe, *What Are They Saying About Biblical Archaeology?* (Ramsey, NJ: Paulist, 1984).

K.M. Kenyon, *Archaeology in the Holy Land* (2nd ed.; New York—Washington, DC: Praeger, 1966).

K.M. Kenyon, *The Bible and Recent Archaeology* (Atlanta: John Knox, 1978).

H.D. Lance, *The Old Testament and the Archaeologist* (Philadelphia: Fortress, 1981).

P.D. Miller et al. (eds.), *Ancient Israelite Religion* (Philadelphia: Fortress, 1987).

J.B. Pritchard (ed.), *Ancient Near Eastern Texts Relating to the Old Testament* (2nd ed.; Princeton, NJ: Princeton University Press, 1955).

J.B. Pritchard (ed.), *The Ancient Near East in Pictures Relating to the Old Testament* (Princeton, NJ: Princeton University Press, 1954).

J. B. Pritchard (ed.), *The Ancient Near East: Supplementary Texts and Pictures Relating to the Old Testament* (Princeton, NJ: Princeton University Press, 1969).

D. Winton Thomas (ed.), *Documents from Old Testament Times* (New York, Edinburgh and London: Nelson; 1958; New York: Harper and Row, 1961).

E.K. Vogel, *Bibliography of Holy Land Sites* (Cambridge, MA: American Schools of Oriental Research, 1974).

M. Wheeler, *Archaeology from the Earth* (Baltimore: Penguin, 1956).

D.J. Wiseman and E. Yamauchi, *Archaeology and the Bible: An Introductory Study* (Grand Rapids: Zondervan. 1979).

G.E. Wright, *Biblical Archaeology* (rev. ed.; Philadelphia: Westminster, 1962).

4. WORDS AND MOTIFS

A. *The Covenant Motif*

ANYONE WHO PATIENTLY reads through the Old Testament will be impressed by the frequent occurrence of the word "covenant" in some of the most obviously significant sections of the Hebrew Scriptures. The term appears in references to God's relationship with his people in the times of Noah, Abraham, Moses, Joshua, David, Josiah, Jeremiah, and Ezra. The great heroes of the Jewish religious tradition emerge as catalysts in the process in which God joins with his people in a covenantal relationship. The word "covenant" is clearly an important part of ancient Israel's religious vocabulary.

Most of the Old Testament was written in Hebrew, a language representing, along with Aramaic, Canaanite, and other languages, the north-west branch of the family of Semitic languages. The early books of the Old Testament were composed in the Phoenician script and later transcribed into the square or Aramaic script. The individual words were first written only in consonants. As is

the case with Arabic today, the reader was supposed to supply the vowels. Hebrew and other Semitic languages rely
on a system of roots, usually consisting of three letters, to
generate the various verbal and nominal forms. For example, the three letters *ktb* involve the idea of writing. Verbs
and nouns that have to do with writing are formed by com-
bining *ktb* with other letters and by leaving clues as to how
this or that form is to be vocalized.

For these reasons and others, the study of words in the
Hebrew Scriptures is a good deal more complicated than it
may seem at first sight. It involves the traditional concerns
of etymology, grammar, and syntax. It can branch out on
the one hand to theoretical linguistics and on the other
hand to ancient Near Eastern history and culture. Rather
than reviewing these complexities abstractly and getting
bogged down in debates over linguistic theory, I suggest
that the major issues involved in the study of an Old Testament word or a motif be raised in connection with the term
"covenant."

The Hebrew word that underlies "covenant" in the
English versions is *bĕrît*. The consonants are *brt,* and the
reader is directed to vocalize the second vowel as a long *i*
by the inclusion of a *y* (yodh) between the last two consonants. All the Semitic languages follow the pattern of
triliteral roots as the building blocks of their words, and
frequently the same roots appear in several languages with
much the same meaning. In the case of *bĕrît,* however, the
comparison of usages in Hebrew with those in other languages is not very helpful.

Where does one go to find out about the meaning of
bĕrît ("covenant")? How did the translators know enough
to render it as "covenant," and how do we know that they
were correct? The treatment of "covenant" in this chapter
will first explore the proposals that have been made concerning the etymology of *bĕrît*. Then it will discuss some of

the most important occurrences of the term, look at its "nonreligious" uses and its ancient Near Eastern background, and sketch its role in expressing God's relationship to Israel as his chosen people. Finally the results of the investigation will be applied to two key Old Testament texts: Josh 24:14-15 as an illustration of "covenant" as a concept structuring the meaning of other words, and Jer 31:31-34 as proof of the vitality of this motif at a time when other key elements in Israel's religious life were disappearing.

An obvious starting point in the analysis of a biblical term is to look at its etymology; that is, the word or words in Hebrew or a related language from which it may have been derived. For the etymology of *běrît*, M. Weinfeld in his article in *Theological Dictionary of the Old Testament* lists several possibilities: (1) the Hebrew verb for "eat, dine" (*brh*) with its suggestions of a festive meal accompanying the covenant ceremony; (2) the preposition meaning "between, among" also found in Akkadian; (3) the verb "to look for, choose" (*brh*); and (4) the noun for "clasp, fetter" associated with the Akkadian *biritu* and carrying the idea of obligation.

Studies of the etymology of *běrît*, however, do not help us very much. No one of the four suggested explanations is entirely satisfactory. One gets the impression that their proponents started from the general knowledge of the meaning of *běrît* and searched for evidence that might emphasize the particular aspect that they thought was most important—meal, relationship, selection, or obligation. Furthermore, we all know from everyday experience that the meaning of words can change radically. They often outgrow the meaning of their original components. To expect that the earliest meaning of a term will be present in every one of its uses over the centuries is simply wrongheaded. However fascinating that it may be, etymology is often very speculative and is not necessarily a good guide to the meaning of a term in a particular instance.

A more promising avenue of approach is the examination of some important texts in which the word *běrît* is prominent. A list of Old Testament passages in which a particular term occurs is supplied by a concordance. There are concordances to the Hebrew Bible and the ancient Greek Septuagint as well as to several of the modern English translations. The concordance usually supplies several words of the context in which the term appears in any particular instance.

One who consults a concordance in search of information about *běrît* or "covenant" will find that the word is used in the description of the promise to Noah that God would never again destroy all flesh by a flood (Gen 9:8-17). The covenant with Abraham narrated in Genesis 17 is like the one made with Noah in that it conveys an unconditional promise, but it differs in that its focus is narrowed down to Abraham and his descendants and it concerns the land of Canaan. The earlier version of the story about God's covenant with Abraham in Genesis 15 includes some kind of ceremony in which animals are cut up and used symbolically. From these texts the following aspects of "covenant" emerge: It is an agreement expressing God's relationship to people and especially to his chosen people. It may be accompanied by a symbolic ceremony. The usual idiom is "to cut a covenant," an expression that may have something to do with the "cutting" of sacrificial animals in the covenant ceremony, as in Genesis 15.

Another important Old Testament passage in which the term "covenant" is especially prominent is Exodus 19—24, which recounts the meeting between God and Moses on Mount Sinai. First of all, God reminds Israel of what he has done for it: "You have seen what I did to the

Egyptians, and how I bore you on eagles' wings and brought you to myself" (Exod 19:4). In this case the relationship involved between God and his people appears to be conditional on the people's observance of certain stipulations: "If you will obey my voice and keep my covenant, you shall be my own possession among all peoples" (Exod 19:5). Thus the Ten Commandments (Exod 20:2-17) and the various legal cases and calendar regulations (Exod 21:1—23:19) are placed in the context of God's covenant relationship with his people. As was the case with Noah and Abraham, God is clearly the dominant figure in the relationship. But at Sinai the relationship is conditional upon Israel's obedience to the commandments and ordinances. After the promises and threats in Exod 23:20-33, the Sinai covenant is concluded with a public ceremony (Exod 24:1-11). On hearing from Moses the stipulations of the covenant, the people answer with one voice: "All the words which the Lord has spoken we will do." This is followed by the offering of sacrifices, the sprinkling of blood on the altar, the public reading of the book of the covenant, and a meal.

The "book of the covenant" in Exodus 19—24 appears to have a definite structure: a historical prologue describing what God has done for his people and the conditional nature of their relationship (Exod 19:4-6), the stipulations that structure that relationship (20:1-23:19), the promises and threats (23:20-33), and the concluding ceremonies (24:1-11). This outline might be explained as the achievement of one clever editor if it were not for the fact the entire book of Deuteronomy appears to be structured according to a similar outline: history (chaps. 1—11), laws (12:1—26:15), mutual obligations (26:16-19), and concluding blessings and curses (chaps. 27—29). Not only is the word "covenant" prominent in Deuteronomy, but the elements already seen in other covenant passages seem to have furnished the principles according to which the whole book was shaped. The connection between Deuteronomy and the covenant under King Josiah (2 Kings 23) has long been recognized. This Sinai-Deuteronomy model of covenant with its emphasis on the people's obligations was taken up in post-exilic times under Ezra (see Ezra 10:3), who decreed that a covenant had to be made according to which non-Jewish wives and their offspring were to be sent away.

Covenant language is also prominent in references to the relationship between God and David's descendants: "I will be his father, and he shall be my son" (2 Sam 7:14). Again God is clearly the superior, and David is the recipient of a promise that seems to have no conditions: "I have made a covenant with my chosen one, I have sworn to David my servant, I will establish your descendants forever, and build your throne for all generations" (Ps 89:3-4). But in Ps 132:12 the Davidic covenant appears subject to the same kind of conditions as the Sinai covenant: "If your sons keep my covenant and my testimonies which I shall teach them, their sons also forever shall sit upon your throne." The conditional character of the Davidic covenant is also stressed by 1 Chr 28:7: "If he continues resolute in keeping my commandments and my ordinances, as he is today."

Up to this point we have traced the covenant motif as it appears in several important biblical passages that concern God's relationship with his people. The incidents chosen for discussion might give the impression that "covenant" is a theological or strictly religious term. In fact, "covenant" is a prominent secular term used in a wide variety of Old Testament contexts to describe an agreement or an alliance. It can refer to an alliance between leaders or peoples, the relationship between a king and his subjects, an agreement between a military leader and his soldiers, the friendship existing between David and Jonathan, and even the relationship of married people. In other words, the key term in the Old Testament tradition for describing the relationship existing between God and his people was one that was an integral part of Israel's everyday life. The relationship between God and his chosen people was expressed in light of a political analogy, and political and other alliances were interpreted in light of the covenantal relationship existing between God and his people.

The secular background of the covenant motif has been greatly illuminated with the discovery of treaty documents from the ancient Near East. The most complete covenants come from the Hittites in the second millennium B.C. Though the Hittites were not Semites and their homeland was in present-day Turkey far to the west of Palestine, they were very influential in Israel's history (see Gen 23:10;2 Samuel 11) and in the life of other ancient Semitic peoples of the Near East. Less extensive treaty documents from Old Testament times, written in Semitic languages, confirm that the covenant pattern seen in the Hittite treaties was widespread and of long duration.

The ancient covenants were treaties or alliances between leaders on behalf of their peoples. When those entering into the agreement were on an equal footing, the covenant is called a parity treaty ("on a par" or equal level). When one party was clearly the superior and made demands on the weaker party and guaranteed protection, the relationship is described as a suzerainty treaty. The stronger party is the suzerain or lord, and the weaker party is the vassal or servant. The suzerainty treaties may include the following elements: the preamble in which the parties are identified, the historical prologue in which the lord reviews what he has done for the servant, the stipulations that the parties will have to observe in the future with special emphasis on what the vassal must do, the provisions for depositing the document for safekeeping and for reading it on certain occasions, the list of divine and human witnesses, and concluding blessings and curses.

It is not surprising that when these ancient documents came to light, Old Testament interpreters hastened to find the outlines of the suzerainty treaty in specific passages such as Exodus 19—24 and Joshua 24. The problem is always that one or more of the essential elements is absent, and indeed the attempt at finding the entire covenant form in the Old Testament seems forced and artificial. But failure to find the covenant form as a whole does not mean that the covenant motif is absent or unimportant. Just the opposite is true! So pervasive and so fundamental was the covenant relationship in ancient Israel's political and religious life that there was no need to make it explicit or to explain in any great detail. The covenant relationship between God and his people was taken for granted. It was the basic axiom of Israel's religious experience and tradition.

The discovery of the ancient Near Eastern treaties and the recognition of the pervasive character of the covenant motif in Israel's life have sharpened our understanding of Old Testament religion. The treaties show that many key terms and ideas in the religious vocabulary of Israel have their context in the covenant motif: the acknowledgement of God as Lord, the recognition of Israel as God's servants, the interest in God's mighty acts on behalf of his people, the willingness to assume the obligations laid down by the Lord, the understanding that punishments would result if the stipulations of the covenant were not carried out faithfully, and so forth.

Even simple words like "know" "fear," "love," and "serve" reflect the stance of the servant or vassal before his lord in covenant. Other terms such as "steadfastness," "fidelity," "righteousness," and "justice" belong to the vocabulary of the ancient covenants. Recurrent features in

Israel's public worship such as blessings and curses, sacrifices and meals in common, and the calling on heaven and earth as witnesses reflect the context of God's covenant with his people. The prophets criticized the people for breaking the covenant and urged them to mend their ways. They depicted God as a lord calling his servants to account for their actions in a kind of covenant lawsuit (see Mic 6:1-5). The destruction of Jerusalem and the exile of the people in 587 B.C. was interpreted as just punishment for Israel's failures to live up to its covenant obligations, and the first stirrings of hope for renewal were expressed in terms of a "new covenant" (Jer 31:31) and an everlasting covenant" (Isa 55:3). The importance of the covenant motif for understanding the New Testament (or New Covenant) needs no lengthy explanation here.

This discussion of covenant or *běrît* has ranged far and wide, but now it is time to return to the method of studying a word or a motif. In analyzing an Old Testament word, the first step is to find out its Hebrew form and the root meaning of the word. The comparison of the Hebrew word with cognates in other Semitic languages is often helpful, but the search for the etymology of the word is frequently speculative and is not necessarily a trustworthy guide for the interpreter. The root, the cognates in other languages, and the etymology are supplied in *lexicons* of Old Testament Hebrew.

The second step is to work through the occurrences of the term. A list of all the occurrences with several words of context is supplied by a *concordance*. In the case of "covenant" we found that the term is used frequently both in secular contexts and in religious contexts. In the Old Testament it describes God's relationship with his chosen people and appears in connection with the major characters in Israel's religious tradition. A political analogy is being used to articulate how Israel experienced the action of God in its life and worship.

The third step in studying a biblical term involves organizing the occurrences into categories or classes. This too is done in biblical lexicons but to a preeminent degree in a *theological dictionary* or *encyclopedia* of the Old Testament. The advantage of the latter format is that its entries need not confine themselves to individual words but can show how the individual word functions as part of the whole web of meanings. For example, an article on covenant in a theological dictionary of the Old Testament would also treat the many terms related to it ("love," "servant," "lord," etc.) and point out the power of the word *bĕrît* as a motif or an organizing concept for many aspects of ancient Israel's religious vocabulary. A theological dictionary should also discuss the meaning of the term in extrabiblical documents and make readers sensitive to the changes and flexibility present in a word's history.

B. Covenant Texts

1. *Joshua 24:14-15.*   The last chapter in the book of Joshua tells the story of the gathering of all the tribes of Israel at Shechem shortly before the death of Joshua. The ceremony that takes place is described as the making of a covenant: "So Joshua made a covenant with the people that day..." (v. 25). The first part of Joshua's discourse recounts the Lord's mighty acts on behalf of his people from the time of the patriarchs (vv. 2-4), through the escape from Egypt (vv. 5-7) and the wars against the kings on the other side of the Jordan (vv. 8-10), to the gift of the land (vv. 11-13). God has shown his power in his deeds on his people's behalf, and now in vv. 14-15 Israel is challenged in the following terms:

[14]"Now therefore fear the Lord, and serve him in sincerity and in faithfulness; put away the gods which your fathers served beyond the River, and in Egypt, and serve the Lord. [15]And if you be unwilling to serve the Lord, choose this day whom you will serve, whether the gods your fathers served in the region beyond the River, or the gods of the Amorites in whose land you dwell; but as for me and my house, we will serve the Lord."

The language of this challenge illustrates how central the covenant motif was to Israelite religion. In the context of Joshua 24, which is explicitly labeled as a covenant ceremony, the people are being asked to accept Yahweh the God of Israel as their lord. The "fear" expected from the people is the respect owed to their suzerain, and the people are asked to join with Joshua in the task of "serving" their lord. This covenant service is to be carried out in sincerity and faithfulness, attitudes that befit the less powerful party in the covenant relationship. Acceptance of the covenant relationship with Yahweh precludes similar relationships with other gods: "Put away the gods which your fathers served beyond the River..."

The covenant motif not only generates the language used in Joshua 24 but also explains certain structural features in the chapter. The recital of God's deeds on behalf of Israel in vv. 2-13 calls to mind the historical prologues in the ancient Near Eastern suzerainty treaties. The dialogue in which Joshua challenges the people to accept Yahweh as its lord implies the existence of a public ceremony in which the master-servant relationship is explained and ratified. The statement that Joshua made "statutes and ordinances" for the people at Shechem (v. 25) clearly refers to the stipulations of the covenant. The account ends with Joshua's writing down the terms of the covenant and setting up a stone in the sanctuary at Shechem (vv. 26-27)—actions corresponding to the depositing of the covenant for safekeeping and implying that covenant-renewal ceremonies were to be held at regular intervals. This description of the ceremony in Joshua 24 illustrates how fundamental the covenant was to Israel's religious vocabulary and religious life.

2. *Jeremiah 31:31-34.* The prophet Jeremiah was active in Jerusalem during the years before the destruction of the temple in 587 and shortly thereafter. The famous "new covenant" passage appears in a collection of hopeful prophecies gathered together in Jeremiah 30—33, a section that is sometimes called the Book of Consolation. In the midst of the darkest period in ancient Israel's history, Jeremiah consoles the people in the language of covenant:

> [31]"Behold, the days are coming, says the Lord, when I will make a new covenant with the house of Israel and the house of Judah, [32] not like the covenant which I made with their fathers when I took them by the hand to bring them out of the land of Egypt, my covenant which they broke though I was their husband, says the Lord. [33]But this is the covenant which I will make with the house of Israel after those days, says the Lord: I will put my law within them, and I will write it upon their hearts; and I will be their God, and they shall be my people. [34]And no longer shall each man teach his neighbor and each his brother, saying, 'Know the Lord,' for they shall all know me, from the least of them to the greatest, says the Lord; for I will forgive their iniquity, and I will remember their sin no more."

The passage blames the present sufferings of Israel on the fact that it broke the Sinai covenant. God had proved his love in bringing the people out of Egypt and offered it a relationship of great intimacy as lord or husband (v. 32). But Israel's failure to observe the covenant stipulations constituted the breach of that covenant, and the punishments of destruction and exile were deserved. Nevertheless, Jeremiah holds out the possibility of a new and even better covenantal relationship with God.

The basis of the new covenant is God's willingness to forgive the sins of the people (v. 34). The new relationship of covenant will be so overwhelming that its stipulations are to become part of each person's inner life. There will be no need of teachers, for all the people will know Yahweh as their lord (vv. 33-34). Faith in its covenant relationship with God allowed Israel to survive the end of the monarchy and the destruction of the temple. Texts such as Jer 31:31-34 are eloquent witnesses to the power of the covenant motif in the life of God's people.

Summary. The study of Old Testament words and motifs considers the root meaning and etymology (lexicons), the various occurrences (concordances), and the range of meanings and historical settings (encyclopedias and theological dictionaries). The term "covenant" is prominent in the most important moments of Israel's history and serves as an organizing concept or motif for much of its religious vocabulary.

Bibliography: *Words and Motifs*

P.J. Achtemeier (ed.), *Harper's Bible Dictionary* (San Francisco: Harper & Row, 1985).

J.B. Bauer (ed.), *Sacramentum Verbi: An Encyclopedia of Biblical Theology* (New York: Crossroad, 1981).

G.J. Botterweck and H. Ringgren (eds.), *Theological Dictionary of the Old Testament* (Grand Rapids: Eerdmans, 1974-).

F. Brown, S. R. Driver, and C. A. Briggs (eds.), *A Hebrew and English Lexicon of the Old Testament* (Oxford: Clarendon, 1907).

G. A. Buttrick (ed.), *The Interpreter's Dictionary of the Bible: An Illustrated Encyclopedia* (4 vols.; Nashville—New York: Abingdon, 1962); *Supplementary Volume* (Nashville: Abingdon, 1976).

J. W. Ellison (ed.), *Nelson's Complete Concordance of the Revised Standard Version Bible* (New York—Toronto—Edinburgh: Thomas Nelson & Sons, 1957).

H. S. Gehman (ed.), *The New Westminster Dictionary of the Bible* (Philadelphia: Westminster, 1970).

S. Hartdegen (ed.), *Nelson's Complete Concordance of the New American Bible* (Collegeville, MN: Liturgical Press, 1977).

L. F. Hartman (ed.), *Encyclopedic Dictionary of the Bible* (New York—Toronto—London: McGraw-Hill, 1963).

D. R. Hillers, *Covenant: The History of a Biblical Idea* (Baltimore: Johns Hopkins, 1970).

W. L. Holladay (ed.), *A Concise Hebrew and Aramaic Lexicon of the Old Testament* (Grand Rapids: Eerdmans, 1971).

X. Léon-Dufour (ed.), *Dictionary of Biblical Theology* (2nd ed.; New York: Seabury, 1973).

S. Mandelkern, *Veteris Testamenti Concordantiae Hebraicae atque Chaldaicae* (Graz: Akademische Druck-und Verlagsanstalt, 1955).

S. B. Marrow, *Basic Tools of Biblical Exegesis: A Student's Manual* (rev. ed.; Rome: Biblical Institute Press, 1978).

D. H. McCarthy, *The Old Testament Covenant* (Richmond, VA: John Knox, 1972).

J. L. McKenzie, *Dictionary of the Bible* (Milwaukee: Bruce, 1965).

J. F. A. Sawyer, *Semantics in Biblical Research: New Methods of Defining Hebrew Words for Salvation* (London: SCM, 1972).

5. FORM CRITICISM

A. Form Criticism in General

THE TERM "form criticism" can seem quite mysterious to beginners in biblical studies until they recognize how much a part of their everyday experience this operation is. A daily newspaper contains a variety of literary forms: news story, editorial, obituary, recipe, box-score, book review, and so forth. These different items follow relatively fixed formal patterns, and anyone with some experience and intelligence can immediately distinguish one from another. The very form in which the various items are presented already communicates a good deal of information.

In biblical studies, form criticism concerns itself with the formal devices of communication in the traditions or sources used by the biblical writers. It seeks to discover the units of tradition, to describe their formal characteristics, to determine their intent, and to offer some clues to the setting in which the form was used (e.g., worship, school). Form criticism has a literary dimension (the isolation and description of the modes of communication) and a historical dimension (the determination of the form's setting in the life of the community). The historical dimension is not always a possibility for the form critic.

Were the units of tradition oral or written? In any given case that question is not easy to answer, and it is wise always to reckon with both possibilities. The claims of some Scandinavian scholars that practically everything was in oral form until Israel's return from the Babylonian exile are accepted by very few Old Testament specialists. The extreme character of these claims, however, does bring out the point that the milieu that produced the Bible was very much an oral culture. Writing materials were crude and cumbersome by today's standards, and there were no printing presses or copying machines.

An oral culture is a traditional culture, one in which compositions in oral form can be handed on from generation to generation with great accuracy. There are certainly oral elements in the biblical tradition. But it seems just as likely that there are written elements also. Inscriptions from pre-exilic times have been found in Palestine, and there is no reason to believe that writing and reading were very unusual. Oral traditions and written traditions most likely existed side by side. For example, those who recited the Psalms probably did so from memory, but this does not exclude the existence of a written text also.

B.   *Narrative Forms*

The Old Testament is full of good stories—good not only in their power for religious inspiration but also in the artistic skill with which they are told. There are stories about the beginning of the world and the human race, the great ancestors of Israel, the escape from slavery in Egypt, the conquest of the land of Canaan, the exploits of judges and kings, the destruction of Jerusalem, the restoration of the temple, and the triumphs of Daniel and Esther in the courts of foreign kings. Rather than talking about the forms of all these stories, I prefer to focus on one kind of narrative—the call—in the hope of illustrating the values and limitations of form criticism. This discussion will prepare for more general remarks on legal, poetic, wisdom, and prophetic forms of speech.

When the Midianites were causing great trouble for the people of Israel after the entrance into the land of Canaan, the task of defending and rescuing the people fell to the judge named Gideon. The story of Gideon's call to deliver Israel is told to Judges 6:11-18:

> [11]Now the angel of the Lord came and sat under the oak at Ophrah, which belonged to Joash the Abiezrite, as his son Gideon was beating out wheat in the wine press, to hide it from the Midianites. [12]And the angel of the Lord appeared to him and said to him, "The Lord is with you, you mighty man of valor." [13]And Gideon said to him, "Pray, sir, if the Lord is with us, why then has all this befallen us? And where are all his wonderful deeds which our fathers recounted to us, saying, 'Did not the Lord bring us up from Egypt?' But now the Lord has cast us off, and given us into the hand of Midian." [14]And the Lord turned to him and said, "Go in this might of yours and deliver Israel from the hand of Midian; do not I send you?" [15]And he said to him, "Pray, Lord, how can I deliver Israel? Behold, my clan is the weakest in Manasseh, and I am the least in my family." [16]And the Lord said to him, "But I will be with you, and you shall smite the Midianites as one man." [17]And he said to him, "If now I have found favor with thee, then show me a sign that it is thou who speakest with me. [18]Do not depart from here, I pray thee, until I come to thee, and bring out my present, and set it before thee." And he said, "I will stay till you return."

The story has a clear progression of action. The messenger of the Lord appears to Gideon and tells him by way of greeting that the Lord is with him (vv. 11-12). After an initial objection from Gideon (v. 13), the Lord gives Gideon a commission to deliver Israel from the hand of Midian (v. 14). When Gideon objects that he is from a weak clan and that he is the least in his family (v. 15), the Lord reassures him that he will be with him in battle (v. 16) and accedes to Gideon's request for a sign (v. 17-18). The outline of the story begins with the divine or angelic encounter with the person to be called and consists of (a) the greeting, (b) the commission, (c) the objection, (d) the divine reassurance, and (e) the sign.

Discerning the outline of the call of Gideon in Judges 6:11-18 would be simply the literary-critical task of charting the progress of the story, if the same pattern did not occur elsewhere in the Bible. But the call pattern is repeated in connection with Moses in Exod 3:1-12 and Jeremiah in Jer 1:4-10. In the book of Exodus the angel of the Lord appears to Moses on Horeb, the mountain of God, and calls to him from the burning bush (3:1-5). The angel is suddenly changed into the Lord, who greets Moses by identifying himself with the God of Abraham, Isaac, and Jacob (3:6). After the encounter and the greetings comes the commission that Moses is to go to Pharaoh and bring forth the children of Israel from Egypt (3:7-9). Moses objects: "Who am I . . . (v. 10)?" But God reassures him that "I will be with you" (v. 11) and promises as a sign that Moses and the people will serve God on this same mountain (v. 12). The other elements in the call pattern have been placed before us: commission, objection, reassurance, and sign.

The call pattern occurs also in the story of Jeremiah as it is told in Jer 1:4-10. The encounter and greeting are somewhat truncated, but the story leaves no doubt that

Jeremiah engages in conversation with God. He is appointed to be a prophet to the nations (v. 5), but he objects that he does not know how to speak because he is only a youth (v. 6). The Lord breaks down his objections and reassures Jeremiah that "I am with you to deliver you" (v. 8). As a sign, the Lord touches Jeremiah's mouth and interprets the sign by saying that he has put his words in the prophet's mouth (v. 9). The story of Jeremiah's call shows the same pattern as the calls of Gideon and Moses: encounter, greeting, commission, objection, reassurance, and sign.

What are we to make of the fact that the calls of Israel's liberator and lawgiver, a famous judge, and a great prophet are told in very much the same way? There are no clear indications that Gideon and Jeremiah modelled the stories of their calls on the call of Moses, and the contents of the three stories do not force one to suppose that two authors were copying from a third author. Rather, it seems that this is the way in which the calls of famous religious characters were told in ancient Israel and handed on from generation to generation. It is appropriate to speak of a call or commissioning form that contains the six elements present in the stories of Moses, Gideon, and Jeremiah.

Analysis of the three call-stories represents the first step in form criticism—the isolation of the literary pattern. The second step—determining the setting in life—is not so easy. The call pattern occurs in connection with characters hundreds of years apart, who exercised very different functions under very different social and political conditions. Relating the call narrative to the temple or the prophetic guild or to local shrines lacks solid foundation. Explaining the stories as based on the everyday experience of a superior's commissioning of a servant or subject helps us to understand the dynamics of the dialogue, but touches only a part of the account.

The more satisfactory explanation is that this call pattern corresponds to the nature of religious experience in ancient Israel. As people in ancient Israel tried to articulate what remains ultimately beyond human speech, they struck upon this call or commissioning form as a good way of expressing the dynamics involved in encounter with God. The lordship of God, his entrance into our lives for specific purposes, the acknowledgement of human weaknesses and limitations, and the assurance that God is with us—all these dimensions of the human encounter with God are expressed in these call stories. In this instance the form critic is hard put to come up with a specific setting in life, and it is preferable to look to everyday experience and the dynamics of religious experience in ancient Israel to get behind the written text.

C. Legal Forms

The material in the legal sections of the Old Testament is customarily divided into two major types: apodictic and casuistic. An apodictic law is an absolute statement. No circumstances and no motives are supplied. The classic examples of apodictic law are found in the Ten Commandments: "You shall not kill. You shall not commit adultery. You shall not steal..." (Exod 20:13-17; Deut 5:17-21). Another form of apodictic law is represented by passages like Exod 21:15: "Whoever strikes his father or his mother shall be put to death." A third formula in which apodictic law is expressed is represented by Deut 27:16: "Cursed be he who dishonors his father or his mother." The claim is sometimes made that apodictic law is unique to Israel's religious tradition and that this kind of ruling reflects faith in the absolute authority of Yahweh. But instances of apodictic law are found in ancient Near Eastern documents, though not in such numbers as in the Old Testament. The more widespread legal form is casuistic law. The term "casuistic" refers to the cases or legal precedents on which the laws are based, not to the lawmaker's interest in fine distinctions. Casuistic law has a two-part structure: *if/whenever* the circumstances are such and such, *then* the punishment shall be so and so. This form of law has countless parallels in antiquity and is still used today. Indeed it reflects the essence of the law in that it deals with specific cases and relates the punishment to the case.

An example of casuistic law is Exod 21:18-19: "When men quarrel and one strikes the other with a stone or with his fist and the man does not die but keeps to his bed, if the man rises again and walks abroad with his staff, then he that struck him shall be clear; only he shall pay for the loss of time, and shall have him thoroughly healed." The case involves a fight between two men in which one of them is injured. If the injured man recovers, the aggressor is liable only for the injured party's loss of pay and medical expenses. The case has been stated, and the punishment is specified. No one claims that casuistic law is unique to Israel. Its prominence in the Old Testament shows how much the Jewish legal system shares with the legal systems of its neighbors.

D. Psalms

In the study of the Psalms form criticism has been particularly effective in distinguishing the various literary types and in determining their settings in the life of the community. The result has been to relate the Psalms closely to the worship services carried on in the temple at Jerusalem.

The largest class of Psalms is the *individual lament* in which the speaker in a difficult situation complains about his enemies. The psalms belonging to this category are Psalms 3; 5; 6; 7; 13; 17; 22; 25; 26; 27:7-14; 28;31; 35; 38; 39; 42; 43; 51; 53; 55; 56; 57; 61; 63; 64; 69; 70; 71; 86; 88; 102; 109; 120; 130; 140; 141; 142; 143. The elements present in this kind of psalm are the address to God, the complaint describing the situation, the request for help, the reasons why God should intervene, the expression of confidence in God's ability to help, the affirmation of innocence or confession of sin, and the conclusion.

The so-called psalms of confidence (Psalms 4; 11; 16; 23; 27:1-6; 63; 131) are sometimes associated with the expression of confidence in God's ability to help that occurs in the individual laments. The liturgical setting of these psalms is not entirely obvious, but the *communal laments* (Psalms 44; 58; 74; 79; 80; 83; 106; 125) seem to have been used on fast days and in times when there was a threat of natural or military catastophe. The components of the communal lament are the lament designed to move God to be compassionate, the prayer to avert the calamity, and the certainty that the prayer will be heard.

A third major class of psalms is the *individual thanksgiving* (Psalms 18; 30; 32; 40:2-12; 41; 66; 92; 116; 118; 138) consisting of the introductory expression of praise or thanks, the description of the distress and rescue from it, confession of God as redeemer, proclamation of the thanksgiving sacrifice, and the conclusion. This kind of psalm probably accompanied the offering of thanksgiving sacrifices in the temple.

The *hymns* (Psalms 8; 19; 29; 33; 46; 48; 65; 67; 68; 76; 84; 96; 98; 100; 103; 104; 105; 111; 113; 114; 117; 122; 135; 136; 145; 146; 147; 148; 149; 150) were apparently used at the temple on the great holy days. They contain a call to praise or an affirmation of praise, the body of the hymn in which God's attributes and actions are praised, and the conclusion. A subcategory of the hymn is the enthronement song (Psalms 47; 93; 96:10-13; 97; 99) in which the enthronement of God as king is celebrated. The fifth class of psalms is the *royal psalm* (Psalms 2; 18; 20: 21; 45; 72; 101; 110; 132; 144:1-11) in which the king is a major figure. Besides the five major forms there are wisdom songs, victory songs, communal thanksgivings, etc.

Not every psalm assigned to the five major classes contains all the elements, but in most cases there are enough common elements to know that we are dealing with five distinct ways of expressing prayer to God. The components provide a broad outline in which the content of the particular psalm is expressed, but the discovery of the outline should not distract from what is contained within it. Nevertheless, the recognition that most of the material in the book of Psalms conforms to a limited number of literary patterns is an important achievement toward understanding the content. Furthermore, the recognition that these psalms by and large were used in worship services at the Jerusalem temple supplies more help and direction in efforts at using them today in worship.

E. Wisdom Forms

The basic form for expressing wisdom teachings in the Old Testament is the proverb—a brief statement expressing in general terms the results of long human experience. In keeping with the conventions of ancient Near Eastern poetry, many proverbs consist of two parallel phrases. When the phrases say pretty much the same thing, it is synonymous parallelism: "He who corrects a scoffer gets himself abuse, and he who reproves a wicked man incurs injury" (Prov 9:7). When opposite things are said, it is antithetical parallelism: "Do not reprove a scoffer, or he will hate you; reprove a wise man, and he will love you" (Prov 9:8). Sometimes a reason is given as in Prov 26:4: "Answer not a fool according to his folly, lest you be like him yourself." There are only a few appeals to the nature of God or to Israel's history. The primary concern seems to be getting along successfully in everyday life, with enlightened self-interest as the major motivation.

Wisdom teachings are frequently expressed in comparisons taken over from everyday life: "Like a madman who throws firebrands, arrows, and death, is the man who deceives his neighbor and says, 'I am only joking!'" (Prov 26:18-19). The list is another common form: "Three things are never satisfied; four never say 'Enough': Sheol, the barren womb, the earth ever thirsty for water, and the fire which never says, 'Enough'" (Prov 30:15-16). Besides these more obvious forms, wisdom teachings can be expressed in riddles (see Judges 14:14), in psalms (Psalms 1; 37; 49; 73; 112; 127; 128), and in narratives (Prov 4:1-9; 7:6-23).

The settings in life offered for wisdom teaching cover a wide spread: the family or clan, the schools, and the royal court. Given the international character of most of the wisdom material and the breadth of its concerns, it is difficult to point to a single setting as primary. The wisdom sayings are expressed in a way that made memorization easy, and clearly—as we shall later discuss under the rubric of "source criticism"—they circulated in small units before being collected into whole books like Proverbs, Ecclesiastes, and Sirach.

F. Prophetic Forms

The Old Testament prophets used the wide range of rhetorical devices found in the Wisdom books—songs, questions, similitudes, narratives, etc. But the most distinctive and best-known form of prophetic speech is the prophetic oracle spoken in the name of the Lord: "Thus says the Lord. . ." This form captures the prophet's identity as one who speaks on God's behalf to the people and makes known his will. Most prophetic oracles are short, poetic pieces, full of passion, looking toward the future, and somewhat mysterious. The prophetic books gather together these brief units into anthologies bearing the name of a single prophet. But the prophets did not set out to write books. Rather, their oracles were delivered orally and were memorized by disciples and admirers who eventually produced written collections. This process of transmission was surely accompanied by adaptation and interpretation on the part of the disciples and admirers.

Among the most important forms of prophetic speech are the threat and the reproach, and these two forms frequently appear together as in Amos 2:6-8:

> ⁶Thus says the Lord:
> "For three transgressions of Israel,
> and for four, I will not revoke the punishment."

The oracle is introduced as the word of the Lord and contains a threat that God will indeed punish the people of the northern kingdom for their sins. Then Israel is reproached:

> because they sell the righteous for silver, and the needy for a pair of shoes—⁷they that trample the head of the poor into the dust of the earth, and turn aside the way of the afflicted; a man and his father go in to the same maiden, so that my holy name is profaned; ⁸they lay themselves down beside every altar upon garments taken in pledge; and in the house of their God they drink the wine of those who have been fined.

The reproach contains the reasons why the threat will be brought to fulfillment. The order may be reversed so that the reproach precedes the threat as in Amos 3:10-11:

> [10]"They do not know how to do right," says the Lord, "those who store up violence and robbery in their strongholds." [11]Therefore thus says the Lord God: "An adversary shall surround the land, and bring down your defenses from you, and your strongholds shall be plundered."

Instead of a threat there may be a promise as in Amos 9:11-12:

> [11]"In that day I will raise up the booth of David that is fallen and repair its breaches, and raise up its ruins, and rebuild it as in the days of old; [12]that they may possess the remnant of Edom and all the nations who are called by my name," says the Lord who does this.

The few examples of prophetic speech from the book of Amos illustrate the most important formal features. The units are short and fairly simple. Parallel phrases are used to make the same points in slightly different ways. The threats and the promises will be carried out in the future. The speech is passionate and poetic, and it is not entirely clear when or how these things are to come to pass.

Attention to the reproach, the threat, and the promise as the most distinctive forms of prophetic speech should not obscure the fact that the prophets used many other forms of communication. These other forms included the dispute in which God lays out his case against his people (Isa 40:12-13), the lament in which the prophet bewails the destruction and suffering (Isa 1:4-9; 5:8-25), the exhortation in which the prophet urges conversion and better conduct (Amos 5:4-6), and symbolic actions in which the prophet acts out the prophecy (Isa 20).

Summary. Form criticism considers the range of devices used to communicate and seeks to determine the settings in which the literary forms were used in ancient Israel before they became part of the biblical books. In addition to narrative forms (the call), there are legal (apodictic and casuistic), poetic (the various classes of psalms), wisdom (proverb), and prophetic (threat, reproach, promise) forms of speech. The isolation of the individual literary forms is an important step in understanding the content of the Old Testament. It is not always possible to connect the literary forms with specific settings in Israel's life.

Bibliography: Form Criticism

W. Brueggemann, *The Message of the Psalms* (Minneapolis: Augsburg, 1985).

O. Eissfeldt, *The Old Testament: An Introduction* (Oxford: Blackwell, 1965) pp. 9–127.

H. Gunkel, *The Legends of Genesis* (New York: Schocken, 1964).

H. Gunkel, *The Psalms: A Form-Critical Introduction* (Philadelphia: Fortress, 1967).

J. H. Hayes (ed.), *Old Testament Form Criticism* (San Antonio, TX: Trinity University Press, 1974).

R. Knierim, "Old Testament Form Criticism Reconsidered," *Interpretation* 27 (1973) 435-468.

K. Koch, *The Growth of the Biblical Tradition: The Form-Critical Method* (New York: Charles Scribner's Sons, 1969).

G. Lohfink, *The Bible: Now I Get It! A Form-Criticism Handbook* (Garden City, NY: Doubleday, 1979).

P.D. Miller, *Interpreting the Psalms* (Philadelphia: Fortress, 1986).

E. Nielsen, *Oral Tradition: A Modern Problem in Old Testament Interpretation* (London: SCM, 1954).

G. M. Tucker, *Form Criticism of the Old Testament* (Philadelphia: Fortress, 1971).

C. Westermann, *Basic Forms of Prophetic Speech* (Philadelphia: Westminster, 1967).

6. SOURCE CRITICISM
AND REDACTION CRITICISM

A. *Their Relationship*

JUST AS the recognition of literary forms is part of everyday experience, so are the use of sources and the task of editing or redacting sources into final form. Suppose that you have been appointed to be recording secretary of a committee or social organization. The group wishes to make a proposal to someone in authority. A meeting of your organization has been called, and you have the responsibility to make a report on the issue to those in authority. Obviously you are not going to write the report on your own and entirely out of your own head. Otherwise, you need not bother to go to the meeting. If you want to write a good report, you will gather whatever material exists in writing and take notes on what is said at the meeting. If the written and oral material represents a clear and acceptable position, your task of editing will be easy. If not, then your own intelligence and creativity will have to go to work. Your contribution as an editor or redactor depends to a large extent on how closely you feel able to follow your sources.

The present forms of nearly all the books of the Old Testament reflect a complicated combination of tradition and redaction. The biblical writers lived in a traditional society, with a great respect for the past. Originality of authorship was not an important value, and the use of existing sources was a very common procedure.

Source criticism tries to detect where sources were used in the book. Redaction criticism pays attention to how the sources were used and what the adaptation of the sources tells us about the editor's theological interests. They are really two aspects of one operation. Once the source has been isolated on external grounds (we are told that a source has been used) or internal grounds (the vocabulary and literary style mark the passage off from surrounding material), then it is often possible to see what the biblical writer has done with it (redaction criticism).

B.   *Source Criticism*

Source criticism aims to show the extent to which the present forms of our biblical books reflect the reliance on or incorporation of already existing written or fixed oral material. At some points the biblical writers tell us that they used written sources. In Num 21:14-15 there is a quotation from the "Book of the Wars of the Lord," and in Josh 10:13 and 2 Sam 1:18 there are citations from the "Book of Jashar." Apart from these references, nothing is known of the now-lost books. In 1 Kings there are mentions of the "Book of the Acts of Solomon" (11:41), the "Book of the Chronicles of the Kings of Israel" (14:19), and the "Book of the Chronicles of the Kings of Judah" (14:29). 2 Chr 25:26 refers to the "Book of the Kings of Judah and Israel," probably identical with the books of Samuel and Kings in the canon of Scripture. In the book of

Nehemiah the autobiographical memoirs of the central character are introduced with the phrase "the Words of Nehemiah the son of Hacaliah" (1:1).

The few stray references to written sources in the Old Testament are far from exhausting the subject of the use of existing material by the biblical writers. Our analysis of the legal forms into apodictic and casuistic established the existence of individual units at the disposal of ancient authors. When the legal material is treated from the perspective of source criticism, the question arises as to whether the biblical writer simply put together these individual legal rulings or had access to already formed blocks of laws.

When there is no explicit notice that a source is used, how can one detect the presence of an already existing source in a book of the Old Testament? There are several indicators: a vocabulary that differs greatly from everything else in the book, a sudden shift in literary style or tone, an unexpected interruption of the context and an awkward resumption of it a little later, the appearance of the same story twice in slightly different forms (a doublet), and theological or ideological contradictions within the same book.

It is possible to point to several passages in the Pentateuch that appear to incorporate large sections of legal source material. For example, in the so-called Holiness Code of Leviticus 17—26 there are two blocks of regulations about marriage and sexual relationships (18:6-30 and 20:10-26). The content of these laws is basically the same, and apparently the two sections represent collections taken over almost verbatim by the editor of the Holiness Code. In the Book of the Covenant (Exod 20:22—23:33) the "ordinances" beginning in Exod 21:1 and ending in 22:17 form a separate unit and probably existed as such prior to their uses in the larger portion. The block of case laws in

Deuteronomy 21—25 probably also existed before the book as a whole was formed. These examples indicate that some written sources were used in the legal books of the Old Testament.

That the narrative books of the Old Testament utilized existing sources is easy to see. The vocabulary, literary style, and content of 2 Sam 9—20 and 1 Kings 1—2 suggest that an early account of events connected with King David's court has been incorporated into the larger story of the monarchy. The colorful exploits of the prophets Elijah and Elisha in 1 Kings 17—2 Kings 10 bear the mark of already existing material. For the Chronicler, the books of Samuel and Kings were written sources to be shaped in accordance with the realities and hopes of Jewish life in Jerusalem around 400 B.C. The book of Ezra cites official Aramaic documents in chaps. 4—7, and the book of Nehemiah incorporates the memoirs of Nehemiah. Surely the many lists in Ezra-Nehemiah also reflect the reliance upon written sources.

The narrative parts of the Pentateuch involve some special source-critical problems. The first five books of the Old Testament were most likely put in final form around 550 B.C. during the period of the Babylonian exile. This so-called Priestly edition incorporated older sources and provided a framework that expressed the interests and concerns of the priests. The material added to the older sources in this edition is designated by the symbol P for "Priestly." The book of Deuteronomy, which is the fifth book of the Pentateuch, was probably designed as an introduction to the history of the conquest and the monarchy. It has been given the sign D. The Priestly editors apparently had access to at least two extensive written sources. The earlier source used the name "Yahweh" for God, and so it won the designation J for "Jahwist." This source took shape around 950 B.C., perhaps at the court of King Solomon. The later source called God "Elohim" (the Hebrew word for "gods") and thus is designated as E for "Elohist." The Elohist source was formed around 900 B.C., probably in the court of the king of the northern branch of the divided monarchy. Sometime after the fall of the northern kingdom in 722 B.C. the Yahwist source and the Elohist source were combined into a single narrative. The Priestly editors had access to the combined narrative as a source.

According to the documentary hypothesis outlined in the preceding paragraph, the Pentateuch consists of four major sources: Yahwist (J), Elohist (E), Priestly (P), and Deuteronomist (D). The time-span from the earliest of the four documents (J) to the final form incorporating the Priestly material (P) is about four-hundred years.

The neatness of this documentary hypothesis can mask the fact that the composition of the Pentateuch was probably even more complicated. Surely the Yahwist and the Elohist writers used sources going well back into the second millennium. Efforts at isolating such sources and placing them under a single designation have not won universal approval, but the persistence of such attempts bears witness to the recognition that not everything is explained by the classic documentary hypothesis.

Furthermore, there have been serious attempts at distinguishing strata or levels within the individual sources (J^1, J^2, E^1, E^2, etc.). The main outlines of the documentary hypothesis for the composition of the Pentateuch are fairly well established, but these outlines represent only the general framework in which a much more complex process of tradition is to be located.

The other books of the Old Testament provide even clearer indications that they incorporate blocks of already formed material. The collection of hymns that is called the book of Psalms contains several groups of songs: the songs of ascents or pilgrimage songs (Psalms 120-134), the psalms attributed to Korah (Psalms 42; 44—49; 84—85; 87—88) and Asaph (Psalms 50; 73—83), and the many psalms of David. The present Psalter emerges as a collection of several existing collections.

A similar situation is supposed by the book of Proverbs, where the various collections of sayings are marked off by headings: the proverbs of Solomon (1:1), the proverbs of Solomon (10:1), the words of the wise (22:17), the sayings of the wise (24:23), the proverbs of Solomon which the men of Hezekiah king of Judah copied (25:1), the words of Agur son of Jakeh of Massa (30:1), and the words of Lemuel, king of Massa, which his mother taught him (31:1).

Likewise, the books of the prophets feature collections of oracles spoken in God's name or about God, autobiographical reminiscences about the prophet, and narratives about him as told by disciples. Almost every book in the Old Testament presupposes the use of written sources.

C.   Redaction Criticism

Redaction criticism aims to determine what the person responsible for the book in roughly the form that we know it did with the sources and what these adaptations tell us about the interests and concerns of the biblical writer. The examples studied in this chapter illustrate two different cases of redaction criticism: when both the source and the redaction of it still exist (2 Sam 7:1-17; 1 Chr 17:1-15) and when an entire book has been structured according to a definite plan (Haggai).

1. *2 Sam 7:1-17 and 1 Chr 17:1-15.* An easy entrance into Old Testament source and redaction criticism is provided by

comparison of the two versions of Nathan's oracle to David in 2 Sam 7:1-17 and 1 Chr 17:1-15. The Chronicler in 2 Chr 25:26 tells us that he had access to the "Book of the Kings of Judah and Israel," which is very likely 1—2 Samuel and 1—2 Kings or something much like it. The version of the story in 2 Samuel is very early (about 900 B.C.), while the Chronicler put together his version of Israel's history around 400 B. C. Thus the parallels between 1-2 Samuel and 1-2 Kings on the one hand and 1-2 Chronicles on the other provide a fascinating opportunity to see how someone adapted a five-hundred-year-old text to his own purposes.

Nathan's oracle to David, with its prediction of a temple to be constructed by Solomon and the promise of God's abiding presence with his people, was very important to the Chronicler. When 2 Sam 7:1-17 and 1 Chr 17:1-15 are placed side by side, it is immediately obvious how closely and carefully the Chronicler reproduced his source:

7 Now when the king dwelt in his house, and the Lord had given him rest from all his enemies round about, ²the king said to Nathan the prophet, "See now, I dwell in a house of cedar, but the ark of God dwells in a tent." ³And Nathan said to the king, "Go, do all that is in your heart; for the Lord is with you."

⁴But that same night the word of the Lord came to Nathan, ⁵"Go and tell my servant David, 'Thus says the Lord: Would you build me a house to dwell in? ⁶I have not dwelt in a house since the day I

17 Now when David dwelt in his house, David said to Nathan the prophet, "Behold, I dwell in a house of cedar, but the ark of the covenant of the Lord is under a tent." ²And Nathan said to David, "Do all that is in your heart, for God is with you."

³But that same night the word of the Lord came to Nathan, ⁴"Go and tell my servant David, 'Thus says the Lord: You shall not build me a house to dwell in. ⁵For I have not dwelt in a house since the day I led up Israel to this day, but I have gone from tent to

brought up the people of Israel from Egypt to this day, but I have been moving about in a tent for my dwelling. [7]In all places where I have moved with all the people of Israel, did I speak a word with any of the judges of Israel, whom I commanded to shepherd my people Israel, saying, "Why have you not built me a house of cedar?" [8]Now therefore thus you shall say to my servant David, 'Thus says the Lord of hosts, I took you from the pasture, from following the sheep, that you should be prince over my people Israel; [9]and I have been with you wherever you went, and have cut off all your enemies from before you; and I will make for you a great name, like the name of the great ones of the earth. [10]And I will appoint a place for my people Israel, and will plant them, that they may dwell in their own place, and be disturbed no more; and violent men shall afflict them no more, as formerly, [11]from the time that I appointed judges over my people Israel; and I will give you rest from all your enemies. Moreover the Lord declares to you that the Lord will make you a

tent and from dwelling to dwelling. [6]In all places where I have moved with all Israel, did I speak a word with any of the judges of Israel, whom I commanded to shepherd my people, saying, "Why have you not built me a house of cedar?"' [7]Now therefore thus shall you say to my servant David, 'Thus says the Lord of hosts, I took you from the pasture, from following the sheep, that you should be prince over my people Israel; [8]and I have been with you wherever you went, and have cut off all your enemies from before you; and I will make for you a name, like the name of the great ones of the earth. [9]And I will appoint a place for my people Israel, and will plant them, that they may dwell in their own place, and be disturbed no more; and violent men shall waste them no more, as formerly, [10]from the time that I appointed judges over my people Israel; and I will subdue all your enemies. Moreover I declare to you that the Lord will build you a house. [11]When your days are fulfilled to go to be with your fathers, I will raise up your offspring after you, one of your own sons, and I house. [12]When your days are fulfilled and you lie down with your fathers, I will raise up your offspring after you, who shall come forth from your body, and I will establish his kingdom. [13]He shall build a house for my name, and I will establish the throne of his kingdom for ever. [14]I will be his father, and he shall be my son. When he commits iniquity, I will chasten him with the rod of men, with the stripes of the sons of men; [15]but I will not take my steadfast love from him, as I took it from you Saul, whom I put away from before you. [16]And your house and your kingdom shall be made sure for ever before me; your throne shall be established for ever,'" [17]In accordance with all these words, and in accordance with all this vision, Nathan spoke to David.

will establish his kingdom. [12]He shall build a house for me, and I will establish his throne for ever. [13]I will be his father, and he shall be my son; I will not take my steadfast love from him, as I took it from him who was before you, [14]but I will confirm him in my house and in my kingdom for ever and his throne shall be established for ever.'" [15]In accordance with all these words, and in accordance with all his vision, Nathan spoke to David.

The textual critic will study these parallel texts in the effort to determine what kind of Hebrew text the Chronicler used, and the philologist will examine the vocabulary, spelling, and syntax of 1 Chr 17:1-15 for evidence of the difference between preexilic and postexilic Hebrew. But the redaction critic will look to those points in which the content of the source (2 Sam 7:1-17) has been changed in order to conform to the Chronicler's theological perspective.

The omission of the phrase "and the Lord had given him

rest from all his enemies round about" (2 Sam 7:1) lessens the gap in time between David's dwelling in his own house and his concern about building a temple for the ark of the covenant. The rhetorical question that begins the oracle ("Would you build me a house to dwell in?") in 2 Sam 7:5 becomes a command ("You shall not build...") in 1 Chr 17:4, lest there be any doubt about the impropriety of David's building a temple. The references to Solomon's sins and the punishment for them 2 Sam 7:14 are excised in 1 Chr 17:13, so as not to cast aspersions on David's son. The wording of the promise in 1 Chr 17:14 ("I will confirm him in my house and in my kingdom") makes it clear that God is the real ruler of Israel and that the king holds power in a kind of theocracy. The phrase "my house" in 1 Chr 17:14 describes the Jerusalem temple, not the house of David and his successors.

Attention to these redactional changes should not obscure the Chronicler's fundamental agreement with the content of 2 Sam 7:1-17. He reproduces most of the source without change. Nevertheless, there are clear tendencies in 1 Chr 17:1-15 to idealize David and Solomon and to reassert the kingship of God. This is what we would expect from a writer deeply devoted to the Jerusalem temple and to the religious renewal of Judaism after the return from exile.

2. *Haggai.*   Another way of doing redaction criticism is to look at the final form of an Old Testament book as a whole. This process is sometimes called composition criticism (because it considers the final form of the work as the composition of the redactor) or canonical criticism (because it concerns the canonical shape of the book or the form that the book takes in the canon of Scripture).

The book of Haggai consists of four prophetic oracles about rebuilding the second temple in Jerusalem. Each oracle bears a date "in the second year of Darius the king"

(520 B.C.), which marks off the major sections of the book as it appears in the Bible: 1:1-15; 2:1-9; 2:10-19; 2:20-23. The entire book cannot be reproduced here, but a glance at it shows a variety of forms within the individual sections: rhetorical questions, promise, request for instruction from the priests, etc. There is no reason to think that the prophet Haggai set out to write a book. Rather, everything suggests that someone else gathered his prophetic teachings together into the collection that bears his name.

The person who was responsible for the composition or canonical shape of the book of Haggai, seems to have had in mind a plan that would bring out to best effect the major themes of Haggai's prophecy. The first oracle (1:1-15) connects the failures and miseries of the people of Jerusalem with their lack of enthusiasm for rebuilding the temple. The third oracle (2:10-19) traces the uncleanness and deadness of the people to the defilement and destruction of the Jerusalem temple. Thus the first and third oracles in the book of Haggai share the theme of neglect of the temple as the reason for the present lack of prosperity.

The second oracle (2:1-9) encourages the leaders of Jerusalem by recalling God's presence in leading his people out of Egypt (v. 5) and promises that God will shake again the heavens and earth and all the nations (vv. 6-7). The fourth oracle (2:20-23) also promises to shake the heavens and earth and to overthrow the kingdoms of the earth. The second and fourth oracles use similar imagery and hold out similar hopes for the future with respect to the splendor of the second temple ("greater than the former," v. 9) and to the leader Zerubbabel ("like a signet ring," v. 23).

The overall plan of the book of Haggai is clear: A (1:1-15), B (2:1-9), A¹ (2:10-19), and B¹ (2:20-23). The redactor or final editor of the oracles of Haggai introduced each oracle with a date formula and arranged the four oracles to bring out two major points: the relation of the people's lack of prosperity to their neglect of rebuilding the temple (A, A¹), and the promise that God will soon intervene dramatically on behalf of the temple and Zerubbabel (B, B¹). Not every Old Testament book has as neat an outline as Haggai does, but the attempt to look at an individual book as a whole and with an eye toward its overall structure is always an important task for the exegete.

Summary.   Source criticism tries to establish where the biblical books have incorporated already existing blocks of material. It does so by paying attention to explicit statements that a source has been used and by analyzing the literary style and the content of the various parts of the books. Redaction criticism considers how the sources have been used by the final editor of the biblical book. It may be carried out on the microscopic level (the comparison between 2 Sam 7:1-17 and 1 Chr 17:1-15) or the macroscopic level (Haggai).

Bibliography: Source Criticism and Redaction Criticism

G. W. Anderson (ed.), *Tradition and Interpretation: Essays by Members of the Society for Old Testament Study* (Oxford: Clarendon, 1979).

I. Engnell, *A Rigid Scrutiny: Critical Essays on the Old Testament* (Nashville: Vanderbilt University Press, 1969).

R.E. Friedman, *Who Wrote the Bible?* (New York: Summit, 1987).

D. Knight, *Rediscovering the Traditions of Israel* (Missoula: Scholars, 1973).

S. Mowinckel, *The Psalms in Israel's Worship* (2 vols.; Nashville—New York: Abingdon, 1962).

M. Noth, *A History of Pentateuchal Traditions* (Englewood Cliffs, NJ: Prentice-Hall, 1972).

W. Rast, *Tradition History and the Old Testament* (Philadelphia: Fortress, 1972).

G. von Rad, *The Problem of the Hexateuch and Other Essays* (New York: McGraw-Hill, 1966).

G. von Rad, *Wisdom in Israel* (Nashville—New York: Abingdon, 1973).

J. Wellhausen, *Prolegomena to the History of Ancient Israel* (Cleveland: World, 1957).

R. R. Wilson, *Prophecy and Society in Ancient Israel* (Philadelphia: Fortress, 1980).

7. TEXTUAL CRITICISM

A. *Principles of Textual Criticism*

THE EARLIEST manuscripts of the books of the Old Testament are removed in most cases by hundreds of years from their original form or autograph. Indeed, since most of the literature in the Old Testament gathers traditions from various times and places, it is even debatable whether we can speak at all of "the original text" in the same way that we might speak of the official text of a law or a church document or the final form of a modern novel. For example, the book of Jeremiah circulated in the third century B.C. and afterward in two quite different Hebrew forms, one virtually identical with the text in the traditional Hebrew Bible and the other (much shorter) version hitherto known from the Septuagint and now witnessed among the Dead Sea scrolls. Which of these best represents "the original text" of the book of Jeremiah? It is hard to say.

The goal of Old Testament textual criticism is to clear away the errors that have crept into the Hebrew text during its many centuries of transmission. It tries to get back as close as is possible to the earliest attainable form of the text. Old Testament textual criticism is a very complicated and sophisticated business, and a detailed discussion of it in a practical introduction intended for beginners in biblical studies would be out of place. But even those who read the Scriptures in modern translations ought to be aware of the nature of the texts on which these translations are based and ought to be sensitive to the decisions that the translators had to make. The textual critic of the Old Testament must survey the ancient texts to determine whether there are variant readings reflected in them, decide what was most likely the original reading, and explain away the other readings as intentional or unintentional scribal modifications.

The initial task of the textual critic is to make an inventory of readings that stand some chance of being original. The maxim that the manuscript evidence must be weighed rather than counted, remains valid. It is entirely possible that in a specific instance only one witness is correct and that all the others are based on a scribal error made centuries ago. Each reading must be judged with reference to good sense, philological probability, and the language and context of the document. The argument from the majority of the manuscripts is never decisive.

The first step in developing a sound text-critical argument is to assemble the textual evidence from the Hebrew, Greek, and other ancient versions of the Old Testament. The oldest complete manuscript of the Hebrew Bible is the Aleppo Codex, which dates from the first half of the tenth century A. D. It will serve as the basis for a new critical edition being prepared at the Hebrew University in Jerusalem. The text of the Hebrew Bible (*Biblia Hebraica,* ed. R. Kittel and P. Kahle [1937]; see now *Biblia Hebraica Stuttgartensia,* ed. K. Elliger and W. Rudolph [1977]), that underlies the modern English translations is the Leningrad Codex (Leningrad Public Library MS B 19[a]), which was written in A.D. 1008. That means that there is a gap of some 1,200 to 1,600 years between the "final form" of most books in the Old Testament and the manuscript on which our translations are based. The problem posed by this vast historical distance is lightened somewhat by the very conservative character of the process of transmission. The Hebrew biblical manuscripts that stand in this tradition are called "Masoretic," a term which refers to the activity of the Jewish scholars between the sixth and the ninth centuries who transmitted the consonantal text and added the vowel points.

From 1947 to the mid-1950's fragments of ancient Hebrew, Aramaic, and Greek manuscripts were discovered in the caves of Qumran and other sites near the Dead Sea. Among the most sensational finds were texts of the Hebrew Bible that antedated the oldest complete manuscripts by a thousand years or more. Some of the fragments even carry us back to the third century B.C. but most of the biblical material comes from the first century B.C. and the first century A.D. All of the canonical books of the Hebrew Bible with the exception of Esther are represented. These manuscripts were generally written in the familiar Hebrew square script with vegetable or carbon ink on scrolls made from leather. They give eloquent witness to the variety of biblical texts in use at the turn of the era and suggest that the so-called Masoretic tradition represents only one type of text among several.

The oldest Greek version of the Old Testament is the Septuagint. Traditionally connected with Alexandria in Egypt and containing versions made by various translators in the third century B.C. and later, the Septuagint made it possible for Jews outside of Palestine to read the Scriptures and later became the Bible of the early church. It supplies the primary texts for the deutero-canonical or apocryphal books of the Old Testament, which are part of the larger canon adopted by the Roman Catholic Church. The earliest complete manuscripts available are from the fourth and fifth centuries A.D. Due in part to the Christian use of the Septuagint in religious debates with Jews, the more literal Greek versions connected with the names of Aquila, Symmachus, and Theodotion were produced in Jewish circles in the second century A.D. Later Christian scholars like Origen, Hesychius, and Lucian also prepared revisions of the Septuagint.

The Dead Sea discoveries have also exercised a dramatic impact on the study of the Greek Bible. Scraps of ancient Greek biblical texts have been found at Qumran Cave 4, and a later first-century A.D. scroll of the Twelve Minor Prophets in Greek that is related to Theodotion's revision was discovered at nearby Naḥal Ḥever. In fact, it is clear that some of the revisions of the Greek Bible were based on earlier revisions (e.g., proto-Lucian, proto-Theodotion). Just as important as the recovery of this first-hand textual evidence for the Greek Bible is the recognition that frequently the Septuagint translations reflect a somewhat different Hebrew text from the Masoretic. In other words, the points at which the Greek text diverges from the Masoretic Hebrew text may not always be explained away as poor translation, carelessness, or theological bias on the part of the Greek translator. Examination of the biblical manuscripts from the Dead Sea area has established dramatically that in many cases the Septuagint was simply based on a Hebrew text different from that which is now called Masoretic. This fact means that the evidence in the Greek Bible must be taken very seriously in any attempt at determining the earliest form of the Hebrew text of the Old Testament.

The Old Latin versions, as distinct from the later translation produced by Jerome and called the Vulgate, were based on the Septuagint and first appear in Christian writings in the middle of the second century A.D. Between A.D. 390 and 405 Jerome translated the Old Testament from the Hebrew text, though in many places the influence of the Old Latin tradition is obvious. The initial responses to Jerome's monumental accomplishment were not wholly favorable (especially from Augustine), but finally the Council of Trent in 1546 declared the Vulgate to be the official Bible of the Catholic Church. Since the encyclical or instruction of Pope Pius XII on biblical studies, *Divino Afflante Spiritu* (1943), Roman Catholics are urged to make new translations from the original texts. A new version of the Latin Vulgate has been completed in Rome.

Among the other important ancient language versions of the Old Testament are the Targums (Aramaic translations and paraphrases) and the Peshitta (Syriac) as well as the translations into Coptic, Ethiopic, Arabic, and Armenian. The Samaritan tradition consists of a Hebrew text of the first five books of the Old Testament (Samaritan Pentateuch), a Greek translation of the Samaritan Pentateuch (Samariticon), and an Aramaic translation (Samaritan Targum). Though not nearly as important as Hebrew and Greek texts, these ancient translations of the Old Testament bear witness to the common desire from very early times that people should read the Scriptures in their mother tongues.

Once the textual evidence has been assembled from the most important ancient witnesses, the second and third steps in Old Testament textual criticism—determining the original reading and explaining away the variants—can begin. The two processes are actually different aspects of a single operation. The determination of the original reading must respect the style and context of the document being studied and must be consistent with good sense and the rules of philology.

Two general rules are of some help in determining the

original reading. The first rule is that the more difficult reading is to be preferred. This rule assumes that copyists tend to simplify and smooth out apparently difficult material, and so what may appear more difficult to ordinary readers stands a good chance of being original. Of course, the reading may be so obscure and so difficult as to be nonsense. The second rule is that the shorter reading is to be preferred. This rule assumes that the general tendency of human beings is to expand rather than to abbreviate. Where there is no possibility that material has been dropped out deliberately or indeliberately, the shorter reading may be more original. Whatever the validity of these general rules may be, the reading judged to be original must be able to explain all the variants. In other words, the textual critic must demonstrate how all the other readings can be derived from what has been judged to be the original reading.

In explaining the derivation of the variants from the original reading, the textual critic of the Old Testament calls upon the various types of deliberate and indeliberate changes involved in the transmission of almost any document. Deliberate changes are naturally the more difficult to detect, since they represent the judgment of someone in antiquity that a particular text needed correction. The most common kinds of deliberate changes are removing rare words or potentially offensive expressions, supplying subjects and objects or other words, bringing parallel passages into harmony, joining variants attested in separate manuscripts, and correcting points of grammar or syntax.

The indeliberate changes are much easier to discover and furnish a surer basis for a text-critical decision. In Hebrew texts several pairs of letters look alike (e.g., *d* and *r, w* and *y*) and are easily confused in the process of copying. In the transmission of any text letters or words may be omitted (haplography) or written twice (dittography). When two words with similar or identical beginnings appear in a passage and the copyist skips from the first to the second and leaves out everything in between, the error is called homoeoarchton (similar beginning). Where the endings are alike and the intervening material is omitted, the process is described as homoeoteleuton (similar ending). Other sources of indeliberate error are transposing letters or words, incorrectly dividing words, and including marginal or supralinear comments in the text.

The way in which the Old Testament has been handed on provides the textual critic with a unique set of problems. The earliest parts of the Bible were first written in the Phoenician or Old Hebrew script, but by the third or second century B.C. there was a change to the familiar square or Aramaic script. In both forms of the alphabet only the consonants were supplied. As is the case with modern Hebrew and Arabic, the reader was supposed to provide the vowels. Yet over the centuries it became increasingly common to use some of the consonants as vowel indicators, and sometimes vowel letters were misconstrued as consonants.

There are cases in which it is not possible to determine the original reading of an Old Testament passage. The Masoretic text may have one reading, and a Qumran manuscript or the Septuagint may have another. Both may be equally probable, and all the commentator can do is to describe the situation. This phenomenon stems in part from the point made at the beginning of the chapter. The books of the Old Testament seem to have been handed on in a variety of forms, so that talk of "the original text" may be ultimately meaningless. The various texts may represent the local editions current in Palestine, Egypt, Babylonia, or other centers of Jewish life in antiquity. The original text in some cases may be beyond our grasp.

B.   *Examples of Textual Criticism*

1.   *Deuteronomy 31:1.*   In the introduction to Moses' parting words to the people shortly before his death, the Masoretic text reads: "And Moses went and spoke these words to all Israel." The Latin Vulgate, which is based on the Masoretic tradition, reflects the same Hebrew text. So does the Samaritan Pentateuch. But the Septuagint differs: "And Moses finished speaking all these words to all the sons of Israel." Did Moses go and speak, or did he finish speaking?

A Qumran fragment from Cave 1 containing parts of Deuteronomy (1Q Deut^b) clears up some of the mystery. In agreement with the Septuagint it reads: "And Moses finished speaking all..." The major problem lies in the first verb of the verse, with the Masoretic text having "and he went" (*wylk*) and the Septuagint and the Qumran fragment having "and he completed" (*wykl*). The only difference is in the position of the final two consonants. When the verb is read *wylk*, it means "and he went." When it is *wykl*, it means "and he finished."

Which reading is correct? The Masoretic reading "and Moses went and spoke" is the more difficult, but it is so difficult as to be close to nonsense. The Septuagint and Qumran reading "and Moses finished speaking" makes better sense in the context of the concluding chapters of the book of Deuteronomy. The exact same phrase appears as a part of a transition from one speech to another in Deut 32:45. Furthermore the Hebrew root *klh* ("finish") from which the verb *wykl* is derived appears several times in the book (see Deut 7:22; 20:9; 26:12; 28:21; 31:24; 32:23; 32:45), and so the expression is consistent with the language and style of the document as a whole. It seems that the earliest version of Deut 31:1 read "and Moses finished speaking" (*wykl*) and that the Masoretic reading "and

Moses went and spoke" (*wylk*) arose when the final two consonants were transposed.

The difference in meaning between the two readings is not very dramatic. Nevertheless, the example is instructive on several counts. It warns us not to reject too quickly the variant readings of ancient translations like the Septuagint. It demonstrates that the general rule about preferring the more difficult reading is not always to be followed. It illustrates that around the time of Christ there was some variety in the text of the Old Testament.

2.   *Deuteronomy 32:43.*   Part of Moses' last words to Israel is the old and lengthy poem found in Deut 32:1-43. That poem in the Masoretic text ends with the following words:

"Praise, O nations, his people,
for he avenges the blood of his servants,
and he takes vengeance on his enemies
and atones (for) his land, his people."

The Samaritan Pentateuch and the Vulgate agree with the reading. But a Qumran fragment from Cave 4 (4Q Deutᑫ) has a fuller and somewhat more exotic text:

"Praise, O heavens, his people (or, with him);
and bow before him, all you gods;
for he avenges the blood of his sons,
and he takes vengeance on his enemies
and repays those who hate him
and atones for the land of his people."

A text very similar to that of 4Q Deutᑫ is presupposed by the Septuagint. Again we suspect that the Septuagint depends on a Hebrew textual tradition other than that of the Masoretic text and that it is not simply a paraphrase or a loose translation of the Hebrew. Now with the discovery of 4Q Deut^{q} among the Dead Sea scrolls we have something very much like that Hebrew text. Since the phrase "and bow before him, all you gods" may have been theologically objectionable to some Jewish readers, we can also suppose that here the longer version represented by the Qumran fragment and the Septuagint is the earliest and more authentic.

Summary. The textual criticism of the Old Testament aims to clear away errors in the manuscript tradition in an effort at reaching the most pristine text possible. It assembles the variant readings found in the ancient texts, decides on the most original reading, and explains how the rejected readings arose. The discovery of biblical manuscripts among the Dead Sea scrolls has established the existence of various textual traditions at the turn of the Christian era and indicates that the Masoretic text represents only one among these traditions.

Bibliography: Textual Criticism

D. R. Ap-Thomas, *A Primer of Old Testament Text Criticism* (Philadelphia: Fortress, 1966).

Biblia Hebraica Stuttgartensia, ed. K. Elliger and W. Rudolph (Stuttgart: Deutsche Bibelstiftung, 1977).

F. M. Cross, *The Ancient Library of Qumran* (2nd ed.; Garden City, NY: Doubleday, 1961).

F. M. Cross and S. Talmon (eds.), *Qumran and the History of the Biblical Text* (Cambridge, MA—London: Harvard University Press, 1975).

S. Jellicoe, *The Septuagint and Modern Study* (Oxford: Clarendon, 1968).

S. Jellicoe (ed.), *Studies in the Septuagint: Origins, Recensions, and Interpretations* (New York: Ktav, 1974).

R. W. Klein, *Textual Criticism of the Old Testament: The Septuagint after Qumran* (Philadelphia: Fortress, 1974).

B. J. Roberts, *The Old Testament Text and Versions: The Hebrew Text in Transmission and the History of the Ancient Versions* (Cardiff: University of Wales Press, 1951).

H. B. Swete, *An Introduction to the Old Testament in Greek* (Cambridge: Cambridge University Press, 1902; New York: Ktav, 1968).

E. Tov, "Hebrew Biblical Manuscripts from the Judaean Desert: Their Contribution to Textual Criticism," *Journal of Jewish Studies* 39 (1988) 5-37.

E. Tov, *The Text-Critical Use of the Septuagint in Biblical Research* (Jerusalem: Simor, 1981).

E. Würthwein, *The Text of the Old Testament: An Introduction to the Biblia Hebraica* (Grand Rapids: Eerdmans, 1979).

8. RECENT ENGLISH TRANSLATIONS

A. Seven New Versions

DURING THE PAST thirty years people whose native language is English and others who read English easily have been presented with seven competent translations of the Old Testament. The question is frequently asked: Which one is the best? To this question the only proper response is another question: Best for whom and for what?

The seven new translations have been prepared by committees made up of biblical scholars, literary stylists, and church leaders. Their chief editors and translators include some of the most learned specialists in biblical languages, archaeology, and ancient Near Eastern history. A common procedure has been to have one scholar with expertise in a particular book of the Bible make a preliminary translation; then this is analyzed and discussed in detail by other members of the committee, and the revised version is sent to still other readers for further comments about accuracy and literary style. The task takes many years and costs a great deal of money. The publication of the New International Version (1978) is said to have involved more than one hundred scholars working in excess of 200,000 hours over a period of twenty-five years at a cost of more than two million dollars!

All the new translations are based on the Hebrew text and use the traditional divisions of the text into chapters and verses. Though these divisions came into being quite late in the history of the transmission of the text and sometimes do not correspond very well to the sense of the document, they have become indispensable for efficient communication. Any attempt to alter the system at this time would be foolish. The translations distinguish between prose and poetry by printing poetic passages according to sense lines. To greater or lesser extents they supply textual notes in order to inform the reader about important ancient variants, places where the text is simply unintelligible, emendations introduced into the text, alternate translations, and the inadequacy of familiar but demonstrably incorrect renderings. Other devices commonly used to increase comprehension of the Bible are sense headings for various sections of the text, introductions explaining the nature of the book and its origins, maps, and other factual information. Several of the new translations come in annotated editions with notes that are the equivalent of brief commentaries on the individual books.

Before a comparison of samples from the seven new translations, some general information concerning their sponsorship, translation philosophy, and intended audiences is necessary. The Old Testament section of the *Revised Standard Version* (RSV) was first published in 1952 and consciously stands in the tradition of the King James Version (1611) and its British (1885) and American (1901) revisions. The RSV was made by a committee of Protestant scholars, but a Catholic edition with a full ecclesiastical approval was published in 1966. It follows the philosophy of formal correspondence according to which every effort is taken to reflect the flavor of and the problems in the ancient languages. Because it is a literal translation and stays very close to the Hebrew, the RSV is an excellent choice as a study Bible. The commentaries in the *Old Testament Message* series use the RSV as their basic text. A second edition of the RSV Old Testament is expected to appear toward the end of the 1980's. It will drop the archaic pronouns used in addressing God ("thou," "thee," and "thine") and will try to substitute more inclusive language for the male oriented expressions ("man," "his," etc.) that are traditional in the history of the English Bible.

The *New Jewish Version* (NJV) began to appear in 1962 with the publication of the Torah or first five books of the Old Testament, and in 1969 there were published the translations of Jonah and the five small books read on various holy days (Esther, Lamentations, Ruth, Ecclesiastes, and Song of Songs). The Psalms appeared in 1972, and the volume on the Prophets was completed in 1978. This translation adheres strictly to the traditional Hebrew text. It seeks to answer the following question: What thought did the person who first recorded the words really intend to express? The style of the translation is, on the whole, modern literary English. An effort has been made to retain the imagery of the Hebrew rather than to render it by English equivalents and approximations alien to the biblical world. The NJV is an excellent translation and has much to offer to Christian readers.

The English *Jerusalem Bible* (JB) and the *New American Bible* (NAB) were prepared under Catholic auspices. Published in 1966, the Jerusalem Bible is the equivalent of the French *Bible de Jérusalem,* which appeared in a single-volume format in 1956. The very valuable introductions and notes are direct translations from the French, though some revision and updating has been carried out. The translations of the biblical texts were generally made from the Hebrew and the Greek and compared with the French text when questions of variant readings or interpretations arose. A thoroughly revised version (NJB) appeared in 1985. It corrected errors, retranslated many texts, and incorporated matter from the 1974 revision of the French. The first complete edition of the *New American Bible's* Old Testament appeared in 1970. Prepared under American Catholic auspices but with the collaboration of several distinguished Protestant scholars, this fresh translation is widely used in liturgy and study. It stands closer in literalness to the RSV than to the JB and tries to reflect the order and style of the ancient languages.

Two translations originally published under Protestant sponsorship reflect the philosophy of the dynamic equivalence. According to this theory, the translator first understands the original as precisely as possible and then says again in the language of the translation what the original author was saying in his. Since the thought conveyed in the text is the most important concern, there is no need to reflect the word order and vocabulary of the original. The Old Testament section of the *New English Bible* (NEB) appeared in 1970 and represents the collaboration of British biblical scholars and literary stylists. This version has been criticized for its questionable philological method of using comparative material from other Semitic languages to translate obscure Hebrew words and to discover new meanings for familiar Hebrew words. The Old Testament part of *Good News Bible* (GNB), which is also known as *Today's English Version* (TEV), was published in 1976. Sponsored by the United Bible Societies, the GNB seeks to state the meaning of the original texts in today's standard, everyday, and natural form of English.

The most recent Old Testament translation is the *New International Version* (NIV), which appeared in 1978. It was made by conservative Protestant scholars. Though not as literal as the RSV, it is more intimately tied to the structures of the Hebrew and Greek originals than the dynamic equivalence translations (NEB, GNB, JB) are. It may replace the King James Version in private and church usage among evangelical Protestants. It is ironic that the translation inspired to some extent by suspicions about the theological orthodoxy of the RSV should end up being quite close to the RSV.

B. Comparing the Translations

In the descriptions of the seven new translations reference has been made to formal correspondence and dynamic equivalence as theories of translation. A formal correspondence translation like the RSV tries to be intelligible to the modern English reader while reflecting the vocabulary, word order, and even the obscurities of the original texts. Dynamic equivalence translations like the NEB and GNB (and perhaps the JB also) are concerned to achieve the same effect in a twentieth-century audience as the biblical authors achieved in their audience. Less attention is paid to verbal equivalence, and more effort is put into the total process of communication. Between these two extremes of translation theory stand the NJV, the NAB, and the NIV.

Both philosophies of translation are defensible. For the serious student who wants to get as close to the original texts as possible, a formal correspondence translation like the RSV is recommended. For someone who is reading the

Scriptures for the first time, a dynamic equivalence translation like the GNB is probably the best choice. In fact, it is often illuminating to use several translations at the same time in the effort at becoming more sensitive to the possibilities and problems involved in the biblical texts. The availability of the seven new translations of the Old Testament should be viewed as a splendid opportunity for increased understanding rather than a source of confusion.

There are three stages in the process of translation: determining the text, establishing the meaning, and discovering the best way to state the meaning. How these three stages proceed and what problems are met along the way can be seen from the following two examples.

1. *Psalms 46:10.* The first part of this verse as it is translated in the RSV and NIV contains a familiar phrase: "Be still, and know that I am God." The verse is often cited as a call to prayer and reflection, an invitation to put aside one's cares and to meditate on the nature of God. There are no textual problems, and the second phrase ("and know that I am God") presents no difficulty for the translator. The initial verb, however, does constitute a problem. It is the second person imperative plural of the Hebrew root that means "sink, relax." The form is causative, and so a literal translation would be something like "let go" or "take it easy."

If the text itself offers no serious problem, the meaning does to some extent. One who reads the whole of Psalm 46 soon realizes that it is not the call to quiet meditation for an individual. Rather, it celebrates in the setting of the temple liturgy the power of Israel's God as he dwells with his people in the holy city. It climaxes in v. 9 with a call to look at the works of the Lord, especially in putting Israel's enemies to rout:

"He makes wars cease to the end of the earth;

he breaks the bow, and shatters the spear,
he burns the chariots with fire!"

Then the psalm changes direction, and in v. 10 God becomes the speaker. In the context of the psalm as a whole, what does the first word in v. 10 mean? Is "be still" an adequate rendering, or is something stronger needed?

This question leads us into a third question facing the translator: What is the best way to state the meaning of the opening phrases in Ps 46: 10? The seven recent translations offer the following versions:

RSV : "Be still, and know that I am God."
NJV : "Desist! Realize that I am God!"
JB: "Pause a while and know that I am God."
NAB: Desist! and confess that I am God.
NEB : Let be then: learn that I am God.
GNB: "Stop fighting," he says, "and know that I am God."
NIV : "Be still, and know that I am God."

This is not a very complicated text, but the translations of it are quite varied. All of them agree in the last part: "that I am God." Several different terms are used for the second verb ("know," "realize," "confess," and "learn"), but there is no significant variation in sense. Only the NAB and NEB do not signal the change in speaker by means of quotation marks before the first verb.

The major difference among the seven new versions comes in the first verb. The options run a gamut from the serene "be still" (RSV, NIV) and "pause a while" (JB) through the sterner "let be then" (NEB) to the harsh "desist" (NJV, NAB). The most colorful and extreme rendition is in the GNB: "Stop fighting." And just in case the reader failed to avert to the change in speaker, the GNB inserts a phrase not in the Hebrew text: "he says."

Which of these translations is most appropriate? That is a hard question to answer with any certainty. Perhaps the familiar misuse of the verse as a call to quiet meditation by an individual demands that "be still" and "pause a while" should be avoided. The GNB's "stop fighting" captures the military context but is much more definite than the Hebrew verb warrants. The NEB's "let be then" sounds strange at least to American ears. The rendering adopted by the NJV and NAB "desist" carries the military nuance of the context and reflects nicely the meaning of the Hebrew form. In this instance the translation found in the NJV and NAB seems best to me.

2. *Genesis 1:1-2a.* An even more familiar text than Ps 46:10 occurs in the initial two verses of the book of Genesis: "In the beginning God created the heavens and the earth. The earth was without form and void..." What is in the Hebrew text underlying this translation? The first verb "create" can be taken as describing an action completed by God: "In the beginning God created..." Or it can be read as a process: "In the beginning of God's creating..." The problem arises because the earliest biblical texts were written without vowels, and the two translations reflect different vocalizations of the same three Hebrew consonants. In the first translation Gen 1:1 is an independent sentence and describes God's creation of heaven and earth out of nothing. The second translation takes Gen 1:1 as the introductory part of the unit ending in v. 2 or even v. 3. It could be taken as implying the existence of a formless earth before God's creative activity started.

The second problem encountered in the Hebrew text involves the expression "the heavens and the earth." According to the ancient view of the world the two words include everything there is. Should the translator retain the two different words, or simply say "the universe?" A similar problem recurs in Gen 1:2 with the words translated as "without form and void." Again two words are employed to say pretty much the same thing. But these two words pose a further problem, for they are very rare words in Hebrew and may have some connection with ancient Near Eastern mythological figures. Is the translator obliged to bring out these mythological overtones? Thus the translator of Gen 1:1-2a faces three difficulties: Is it "God created" or "God's creating?" Is it "the heavens and the earth" or "the universe?" Is it "without form and void" or a single word, and what about the mythological allusion?

The seven new translations illustrate various attempts at dealing with these issues:

RSV : In the beginning God created the heavens and the earth. The earth was without form and void...

NJV : When God began to create the heaven and the earth—the earth being unformed and void...

JB : In the beginning God created the heavens and the earth. Now the earth was a formless void...

NAB: In the beginning, when God created the heavens and the earth, the earth was a formless wasteland...

NEB: In the beginning of creation, when God made heaven and earth, the earth was without form and void...

GNB: In the beginning, when God created the universe, the earth was formless and desolate...

NIV :   In the beginning God created the heavens and
        the earth. Now the earth was formless and
        empty...

Three of the translations (RSV, JB, NIV) take Gen 1:1
as a complete sentence, but the other four (NJV, NAB,
NEB, GNB) present it as subordinate to what follows. It is
probably anachronistic to describe this difference in terms
of the philosophical debate about creation out of nothing
(*creatio ex nihilo*). But the two translations do emphasize
different aspects of God's creative activity, with the former
("God created") stressing his sovereign power and the latter ("when God created") calling attention to his ordering
or shaping function. Since the imposition of order upon
chaos was a common theme in ancient Near Eastern creation stories and since Gen 1:1-2a is part of the Priestly
creation narrative (Gen 1:1-2:4a) in which order (seven
days, etc.) is the major theme, there is something to be said
for the second version. In fact, it may be more appropriate
to this context in which God's role as orderer is stressed
than the more familiar rendition.

The other two problems are resolved quite easily. Only
the GNB chooses "the universe" as a translation of "the
heaven(s) and the earth," and this is a clear application of
the philosophy of dynamic equivalence. None of the
translations makes any effort to bring out the possible
mythological overtones in "without form and void." Their
decision was undoubtedly correct. When the Priestly creation story (Gen 1:1-2:4a) was composed, the terms very
likely had no mythological reference and simply described
the chaotic condition brought into order by the creative
power of God. Two translations combine the two words
into a single expression: "formless void" (JB) and
"formless wasteland" (NAB). There is, however, no ap-

preciable difference in the interpretation of the phrase "without form and void" in any of the seven translations.

Summary. Recent years have seen the publication of seven new English translations of the Old Testament under the sponsorship of various Catholic (JB, NAB), Protestant (RSV, NEB, GNB, NIV), and Jewish (NJV) groups. Their philosophies of translation range from formal correspondence (RSV) to dynamic equivalence (GNB). The task of translation involves determining the original text, establishing its meaning, and discovering the best way of expressing the meaning.

Modern English Translations

Good News Bible with Deuterocanonicals / Apocrypha. The Bible in Today's English Version (New York: American Bible Society, 1979).

The Holy Bible. New International Version. Containing The Old Testament and The New Testament (Grand Rapids: Zondervan, 1978).

The Holy Bible Containing the Old and New Testaments. Revised Standard Version (New York: United Bible Societies, 1971).

The Jerusalem Bible (Garden City, NY: Doubleday, 1966; revised, 1985).

The New American Bible. Translated from the Original Languages with Critical Use of All the Ancient Sources (Paterson, NJ: St. Anthony Guild, 1970; revised, 1987).

The New English Bible with the Apocrypha (New York: Oxford University Press and Cambridge University Press, 1970).

The Torah. The Prophets. The Writings. (Philadelphia: Jewish Publication Society, 1962, 1978, 1982).

Guides to English Translations

L.R. Bailey, ed., *The Word of God. A Guide to English Versions of the Bible* (Atlanta: John Knox, 1982).

J. Beekman and J. Callow. *Translating the Word of God* (Grand Rapids: Zondervan, 1974).

F.F. Bruce, *History of the Bible in English. From the earliest versions* (3rd ed. New York: Oxford University Press, 1978).

S. Kubo, and W.F. Specht. *So Many Versions? Twentieth-Century English Versions of the Bible* (rev. ed.; Grand Rapids: Zondervan, 1983).

J.P. Lewis, *The English Bible from KJV to NIV. A History and Evaluation* (Grand Rapids: Baker, 1981).

J.L. Mays, ed. *Interpretation* 32 (1978) 115-70.

D. McCall, ed., *Review and Expositor* 76 (1979) 297-416.

E.A. Nida, and C.R. Taber. *The Theory and Practice of Translation* (Leiden: Brill, 1969).

9. THE OLD TESTAMENT IN CHRISTIAN WORSHIP

A. Actualization

THE CONTEXT in which most Christians today are exposed to the Old Testament is the public worship conducted in the church. In the cycle of Scripture readings prepared in response to the directives of the Second Vatican Council and adopted subsequently by many Protestant churches, the Old Testament has a prominent place. The three-year Sunday cycle of readings contains a passage from the Old Testament as the first of the three major selections from the Bible. Usually the Old Testament reading is chosen to illustrate some point in or provide the background for the reading from the Gospel. The two-year daily cycle makes provision for many Old Testament selections as the first of the two major readings. In both the Sunday and the daily cycles, fragments from the Psalms are frequently used at the beginning and end of the liturgy. Before the Gospel passage is read, the reader and the congregation join in the singing or reciting of several verses from a psalm. This is the so-called responsorial psalm.

Not everyone is pleased with the present liturgical practice regarding the Old Testament. On the negative side, the critics of the Old Testament find the material hard to understand and even harder to relate to their lives. The strange names and the odd incidents put many people off. The problem is particularly severe in an area in which a long and sophisticated religious tradition may exist as, for example, in India. There the teachings of the New Testament may be respected and well received, but the Old Testament can seem narrow, shallow, and unimportant. The suggestion is sometimes even made to substitute selections from the local religious tradition for the Old Testament and to see how it prepares the way for the good news of Jesus Christ.

Enthusiasts for the Old Testament are also unhappy with the present practice. They complain that too often the selections are designed merely to illustrate the message of the Gospel passage and that the content of the Old Testament is not respected on its own terms. In other words, the Old Testament is presented as only a background for understanding the New Testament, at least in the cycle of Sunday readings. The passages are too short and have been tailored only with the Gospel selection in view. Preachers are thereby encouraged to pass over quickly the Old Testament material, and parishioners get the impression that the Old Testament is simply a book of background to the New Testament. Supporters of the Old Testament in Christian worship argue that the treasures of the Judeo-Christian tradition are not being allowed enough space to make a positive impact on God's people today.

Both the critics and the proponents of the Old Testament in the Christian liturgy have important things to say and deserve a hearing. But even within their complaints it is possible to discern the outlines of a positive position regarding the use of the Old Testament in Christian wor-

ship. The Old Testament can teach the Christian community by situating its faith in a historical context, by reminding
it of the social character of that faith, and by insisting on
the traditional dimension of the faith.

In many ways the New Testament is unintelligible apart
from the Old Testament. Though composed in Greek, the
books of the New Testament reflect the vocabulary and
concerns of Judaism in Palestine and the rest of the
Mediterranean world during the first century A.D. The
Old Testament was the Sacred Scripture not only of the
Jewish synagogues but also of the Christian churches. The
titles used in describing Jesus (Messiah or Christ, Servant,
Son of God, Lord, Shepherd, etc.) all had Old Testament
roots. The language used by Paul and other New Testament authors was basically the Greek of the Old Testament
translation called the Septuagint. A major activity in early
Christian circles was the attempt to show how in Jesus of
Nazareth the promises of the Old Testament made sense
and were brought to fulfillment. The Old Testament was
the Bible of the early church, the most formative document
in its life, and an integral part of its worship. If twentieth-
century Christians are ever to understand the New Testament,
they must not cut themselves off from the Old Testament.

The Old Testament also reminds us of the social
character of our faith. Even when God is presented as dealing with individuals in the Old Testament, the individual is
significant only in relation to the fortunes of God's people.
Abraham, Moses, and David are important only because
through them God deals with his people. There is no cult
of personality in Old Testament faith. Furthermore, the
Old Testament insists that God exercises a special concern
for the "have-nots" of society—for widows, orphans,
strangers, and others in economic need. This social concern is grounded in God's ownership of all creation and his
past benefactions to his people, not in a purely human im-

perative to share. Even the Psalms, which often form the starting point of private prayer for Christians, are essentially social documents. They were written for public worship and are still used most appropriately in that context today. When recited prayerfully by a single person or pondered meditatively, the Psalms retain their social or communal character. The individual reflects upon the documents of the praying community and stands within the community of faith even when he or she seems most solitary.

Mention of the community of faith brings up a third contribution of the Old Testament to Christian life and worship. Besides making the New Testament more intelligible and reminding us of the social character of our faith, the Old Testament insists on the traditional dimension of faith. The idea of "tradition" has not been very popular in recent years in some circles. Talk of future shock, the space age, the now-generation, and so on leaves little place for tradition. Even the fascination with ethnicity and "roots" builds on the assumption that the present is dramatically different from the past. Finding one's roots involves a long and arduous search; it is sometimes hard to know where to begin to find one's roots.

For Christians in search of their religious and human roots, the Old Testament is the most appropriate place to begin. There we will find real human beings with great strengths and great weaknesses struggling to respond to God's presence in their lives and in the life of their people. There we will find that religion encompasses all aspects of human life (law, politics, education, culture) and is not set beside or apart from other pursuits. There we will find great models of faith and persons for whom the only fitting response to God is thanksgiving. This is the beginning of the great tradition of faith that has been encouraged and nurtured by the church throughout the centuries. As we move toward the year A.D. 2000, it becomes ever clearer that the Christian church must make every effort to keep that tradition of faith alive and hand it on to the generations to follow. Loving knowledge of the Old Testament tradition is one necessary part of that task.

As concrete illustrations of some of the ways in which the Old Testament can be made actual in the life of the Christian church, I present the texts of two homilies that I preached recently on Old Testament texts. They show how deeply the New Testament and Christian faith are rooted in the Old Testament and how firmly we stand in the tradition of faith that stretches back to the Old Testament. Both homilies concern great figures of the Old Testament. The figure of Jeremiah provides a model for Christians looking forward to the celebration of Christmas and to the second coming of Christ. The figures from Israel's past singled out for praise by Jesus ben Sirach are not so much models of faith as they are reasons for praising and thanking God. The second homily was preached at my father's funeral. I hesitate to put such a personal statement into print, but the occasion forced me to reflect on and express the things that are most important to me in the biblical tradition.

B.   *Examples of Old Testament Preaching*

1.   *Jeremiah 33:14-16.*   In the time prior to Christmas, Christians are presented with many figures from the Old Testament and asked to stand beside them in faith. In one phase of the three-year Sunday cycle a selection from Jeremiah 33:14-16 is paired with an eschatological passage from Luke 21:25-28, 34-36. From a Christian perspective, the Old Testament reading points toward the consolation expected to accompany the Messiah's coming. In the book

of Jeremiah it is part of the prophet's hope for the restoration of Israel's fortunes after the destruction of the Jerusalem temple in 587 B.C. and the exile of Judah's leaders to Babylon:

> [14]Behold, the days are coming, says the Lord, when I will fulfill the promise I made to the house of Israel and the house of Judah. [15]In those days and at that time I will cause a righteous Branch to spring forth for David; and he shall execute justice and righteousness in the land. [16]In those days Judah will be saved and Jerusalem will dwell securely. And this is the name by which it will be called: 'The Lord is our righteousness.'

The passage from Luke's Gospel uses imagery common in the Jewish apocalypses of the time in order to describe the coming of the Son of Man:

> [25]"And there will be signs in sun and moon and stars, and upon the earth distress of nations in perplexity at the roaring of the sea and waves, [26]men fainting with fear and with foreboding of what is coming on the world; for the powers of the heavens will be shaken. [27]And then they will see the Son of man coming in a cloud with power and great glory. [28]Now when these things begin to take place, look up and raise your heads, because your redemption is drawing near."
>
> [34]"But take heed to yourselves lest your hearts be weighed down with dissipation and drunkenness and cares of this life, and that day come upon you suddenly like a snare; [35]for it will come upon all who dwell upon the face of the whole earth. [36]But watch at all times, praying that you may have strength to escape all these things that will take place, and to stand before the Son of man."

Faith in God's Fidelity.   "Behold, the days are coming, says the Lord, when I will fulfill the promise..." The season of Advent is a time of preparation for Christmas. Advent is a four week period in which we prepare to commemorate the coming of Christ at Christmas and renew our faith in his second coming at the end of human history. Unlike Lent, it is not a time of penance and reflection on Jesus' passion and death.

Advent is a time of preparation, and today's Scripture readings show us an important way to prepare ourselves for Christmas. This way is shown by the reading from the prophet Jeremiah and the selection from Luke's Gospel. Both readings urge us to use our religious imagination and look toward the future with hope. Jeremiah wrote in the darkest period of ancient Israel's history. In 587 B.C. the Babylonian army had overrun Jerusalem and destroyed the temple there. Jeremiah had every reason for sadness and despair, but his prophecy here is full of hope and optimism. Despite all the destruction and disappointment around him, Jeremiah looked toward the future and expressed his faith in God's fidelity to his people. God would fulfill his promises. God would raise up the hoped-for descendant of David. God would make his people safe and secure. Jeremiah's optimism rested not on his own natural disposition nor on the facts of the present situation. Rather, he was optimistic precisely because he trusted in a faithful God. In other words, all of Jeremiah's extravagant hopes for the future of his people depended on God's fidelity.

While the selection from Jeremiah looks to the first coming of Christ, the passage from the Gospel of Luke points toward the second coming. That passage describes the second coming in the terms and images that would have been intelligible to people of Jesus' time. The kingdom of God will arrive only after great natural disturbances, signs in the sun and moon, wars between nations, fear and fright. But in the midst of this scenario there emerges the glorious Son of Man, naturally identified by early Christians as Jesus. Whereas the present time was terrifying for Jeremiah and his companions, the future frightened the people of Jesus' age. Yet for all the terror involved in the future, the trust in the coming of the Son of Man was the basis of hope and optimism for the future and the reason for watchfulness and prayer in the present time. Again this hope rested upon God's faithfulness to his people.

Trust in a faithful God—that is the message of the Advent season. Not only do we prepare ourselves to remember the first coming of Christ with all the joy and gladness at our disposal, but we also express our faith and trust in the future coming of Christ at the end of human history. Trust in a faithful God—that is the message of the prophet Jeremiah. Amidst all the desolation and destruction of Jerusalem in 587 B.C., Jeremiah was sure that God would still fulfill his promises and would send the glorious Son of David. Trust in a faithful God—that is the message of St. Luke's Gospel. Amidst all the fears and terrors aroused by expectation of the coming kingdom of God, Luke holds firm to faith in Christ as the Son of Man and urges a course of watchfulness and prayer.

Trust in a faithful God—that is the central theme of the Advent season, and it is something that can bring new liveliness and new zest to our everyday lives. Once we become fully convinced of God's faithfulness, then our lives take on a new spirit of optimism and expectation. Once we fully allow the faithful God to enter our lives, we can take our place alongside the great figures of the Advent season—Jeremiah and Luke, John the Baptist, and Joseph and Mary—as witnesses to a faithful God.

2. *Sirach 44:1-15.* Chapters 44 to 50 of the book of Sirach form a well-knit and distinct division and have as their theme the heroes of Israel from Enoch to the time of Simeon the high priest around 200 B.C. Israel's privilege

in having had these gifts of God is the major theme, and the appropriate response is praise and thanks to God. The prologue to these chapters (Sir 44:1-15) served as the Old Testament reading at my father's funeral:

> [1]Let us now praise famous men, and our fathers in their generations. [2]The Lord apportioned to them great glory, his majesty from the beginning. [3]There were those who ruled in their kingdoms, and there were men renowned for their power, giving counsel by their understanding, and proclaiming prophecies; [4]leaders of the people in their deliberations and in understanding of learning for the people, wise in their words of instruction; [5]those who composed musical tunes, and set forth verses in writing; [6]rich men furnished with resources, living peaceably in their habitations—[7]all these were honored in their generations, and were the glory of their times. [8]There were some of them who have left a name, so that men declare their praise. [9]And there are some who have no memorial, who have perished as though they had not lived; they have become as though they had not been born, and so have their children after them. [10]But these were men of mercy, whose righteous deeds have not been forgotten; [11]their prosperity will remain with their descendants, and their inheritance to their children's children. [12]Their descendants stand by the covenants; their children also, for their sake. [13]Their posterity will continue for ever, and their glory will not be blotted out. [14]Their bodies were buried in peace, and their name lives to all generations. [15]People will declare their wisdom, and the congregation proclaims their praise.

The Tradition of Faith. "Now let us praise famous men, and our fathers in their generations" (Sirach 44:1).

The death of a parent is one of the most shattering moments in any person's life. The death of my father, Florence Daniel Harrington, on Saturday night was especially painful to me because it was so sudden and because we were so close. But when I was allowed to see his body very shortly after his death, the only emotion present and the only one that felt appropriate was gratitude. I could only thank God for this man who had been a gift—a gift to my mother, to me and my brother, to his grandchildren, to his seven sisters and his brother, and to all who worked with him, enjoyed life with him, and prayed with him. He was a precious gift to us all, and now that gift has been taken away.

The Scripture passage that immediately came to my mind and has shaped my prayer during the last few days may seem unusual. It is the praise of the illustrious figures of Israel's history found near the end of the book of Sirach or Ecclesiasticus. It begins with a call to praise: Now let us praise famous men. It goes on to describe and illustrate the deeds of Abraham, Moses, David, the prophets, and other famous heroes of the people of God right down to the author's time around the year 200 B.C. Why is this passage so significant to me? Why does it express my feelings so well? There are several reasons.

First, the passage urges us to see our faith not simply as a matter of individual decision, existing outside the bounds of time and space. Rather, it demands that we Christians see ourselves standing in a tradition of faith—a tradition going back thousands of years and continuing into eternity. It demands that we Christians see our faith as something carried out in everyday life—in the ways that we treat one another and in the way we relate to God. My father was a man of Christian tradition. The principles that shaped and guided his life were the principles of the Ten Commandments, the Beatitudes, and the teachings of Jesus. His style of piety was molded by the teachings of the church and by the best tradition of Irish Catholicism. He hungered and thirsted for holiness, and he did so in the framework of Christian tradition. He knew better than most of us how richly that hunger and thirst for holiness can be filled within the tradition of faith.

Second, the passage presents the characters of the tradition in ways that may not be immediately apparent. When we see characters portrayed in religious texts, we too quickly moralize and jump to the conclusion that we are supposed to imitate those figures. The famous men of Ben Sira's list are not presented in that way. Instead, we are asked to look at those characters and see in them a reflection of God's own glory. The people of our tradition of faith are God's gifts to us. They are witnesses to God's glory and are displays of his greatness. To think that we can imitate them is arrogant and presumptuous. Who are we to imitate the reflections of God's own glory? I looked upon my father as a display of God's glory and greatness. That is why right now the most fitting response for me is to praise God and to thank him for this extraordinary gift.

Third, the passage touches on one aspect of the immortality granted to those gifts of God in the tradition of faith: Their offspring will last forever. We who are his children and his grandchildren carry on the great tradition of faith present in such a splendid way in my father. Whatever is good and Christian about us, in large measure we owe to him. Those who knew him and were touched by his kindness and generosity have been enriched by him. We have also been challenged by him—challenged to be faithful, to be kind and decent, to carry on the tradition of faith that meant so much to him.

Some time ago I heard a saying that means a great deal to me: If you want to stand in the tradition of faith, you must earn your place in it. My father earned his place in the tradition of faith and embodied it in an extraordinary way. Perhaps few can imitate his hunger and thirst for holiness. But at least we can carry on and keep alive the tradition of faith that was so vital to this gift of God to us.

Summary. The Old Testament can teach the Christian community assembled in worship by situating its faith in a historical context, by reminding it of the social character of that faith, and by insisting on the traditional dimension of the faith. The great figures of the Old Testament provide models of faith (Jeremiah) and reasons for praising God (Sirach).

Bibliography: *Worship*

E. Achtemeier, *The Old Testament and the Proclamation of the Gospel* (Philadelphia: Westminster, 1977).

E. Best, *From Text to Sermon: Responsible Use of the New Testament in Preaching* (Atlanta: John Knox, 1978).

B. S. Childs, *Old Testament Books for Pastor and Teacher* (Philadelphia: Westminster, 1977).

G. J. Dyer (ed.), *The Pastoral Guide to the Bible* (Mundelein, IL: Civitas Dei, 1978).

D. E. Gowan, *Reclaiming the Old Testament for the Christian Pulpit* (Atlanta: John Knox, 1980).

L. E. Keck, *The Bible in the Pulpit: The Renewal of Biblical Preaching* (Nashville: Abingdon, 1978).

G. T. Montague, "Hermeneutics and the Teaching of Scripture," *Catholic Biblical Quarterly* 41 (1979) 1–17.

S. M. Schneiders, "Faith, Hermeneutics, and the Literal Sense of Scripture," *Theological Studies* 39 (1978) 719–736.

J. D. Smart, *The Strange Silence of the Bible in the Church* (Philadelphia: Westminster, 1970).

D. Stuart, *Old Testament Exegesis. A Primer for Students and Pastors* (Philadelphia: Westminster, 1980).

G. von Rad, *Biblical Interpretations in Preaching* (Nashville: Abingdon, 1977).

J. N. M. Wijngaards, *Communicating the Word of God* (Great Wakering, UK: Mayhew-McCrimmon, 1978).

10. THE OLD TESTAMENT IN CHRISTIAN THEOLOGY

A. The Problems of Old Testament Theology

THE PRECEDING chapter on the place of the Old Testament in public worship has already made the jump from the past to the present. Its experiential and practical approach to the question of the abiding significance of the Old Testament provides an entrance into a set of very difficult problems: How is the Old Testament to be used in Christian theology? Is there a theme or concept that unifies the collection of documents that we call the Bible? What is the authority of the Old Testament?

This whole chapter will explain those questions and suggest some answers to them. First it sketches the various approaches used in the discipline called the theology of the Old Testament. Then it proposes as the overarching theme for the Bible the idea of God's relationship with his chosen people. Finally it explores the issue of the authority of the Old Testament for the Christian church today. These issues are very complicated, and my positions are far from definitive. What is most significant is to see that my basic points grow out of the treatment of the methods of Old Testament interpretation discussed in the first nine chapters of this book.

About two-hundred years ago theologians in Germany began to discuss the possibility of developing a truly biblical theology. The idea was to clarify the basic concepts in the Bible and to place these at the service of a renewed systematic theology. The task is noble, but how to carry out the task remains problematic.

The chief obstacle is the nature of the Bible. The Old Testament includes early poems from the twelfth century B.C. (Exodus 15) and books from shortly before Christ's time (Daniel, Sirach, 1–2 Maccabees, Wisdom). The New Testament represents a much more compressed period of time, but it covers a geographical expanse from Jerusalem to Rome. Furthermore, the biblical writers expressed themselves in a wide variety of literary forms: poems, narratives, wisdom sayings, prophetic oracles, etc. The Bible is a collection of writings, an anthology—not a unified theological treatise. The growth of this collection into the present-day canons of Scripture was a complicated process, and by no stretch of the imagination was theological purity the only determining factor. The historical nature and anthological character of the Bible are formidable obstacles in the way of anyone who wishes to work out the theology of the Old Testament.

One strategy in Old Testament theology is to determine what the Old Testament says about God, humanity, sin, grace, law, etc. The crude application of this method involves going through the Old Testament, noting what is said about these themes, and synthesizing the data into the biblical doctrine of the individual topic. The difficulty with this approach to biblical themes is that it treats the Old Testament as a single document representing one viewpoint and flattens out the differences of time and perspective found in the various documents.

The more sophisticated application of the thematic approach respects what the individual documents say about the topic, listens as carefully and accurately as possible to the many voices within the canon of Scripture, and points out the abiding theological significance of the biblical perspectives. This is an acceptable and popular way of doing biblical theology. Despite the harsh criticisms of it and even the premature announcements of its demise, this thematic approach to biblical theology continues to generate many fine books and articles every year.

The special risk that this approach runs in addition to those already cited lies in the themes chosen for study. Too often the agenda is set by the thought categories of eighteenth and nineteenth century Protestant or Catholic theology, and the task is perceived as discovering what the various biblical writers had to say about God, humanity, sin, grace, law, etc. But those categories are not necessarily the thought categories of Scripture. For example, we may be interested in knowing what the Bible says about God "in himself." But the evidence is practically nonexistent, because the Scriptures are really concerned only with God in relation to his people.

The recognition that the books of the Bible must be taken on their own terms and in their own theological framework has led to the descriptive approach to Old Testament theology. Here the task is to work out an accurate description of what was important to the writers of the individual books or to the traditions within the books. Every effort is taken to make the description as objective as possible, and no theological commitment is demanded from the one doing the describing. When all the material in the Old Testament has been subjected to this approach, the result is the history of Israel's religion—a purely descriptive presentation of the theological thoughts of the individual writings and traditions contained in the Old Testament.

The "history of Israel's religion" approach has the advantage of focusing attention on the thought categories and framework of the biblical books. Its emphasis on the descriptive aspect of Old Testament theology is sound. Unless we understand and respect what the basic documents of Jewish and Christian faith say, we cannot begin to find in them guidance and illumination for the present. But many proponents of this approach wish to stop at the task of description and refuse to go beyond it. They maintain that any attempt to pass on from theological description is illegitimate.

The theoretical issues involved in such a stance are varied and complex, but the whole thrust of the Judeo-Christian tradition points in an opposite direction. According to that tradition, the Old Testament is the document of the believing community and comes alive in its worship and everyday life. Carried on within the community of faith, biblical exegesis not only describes the religion of the Old Testament author but also indicates how the biblical documents can shape and guide the religious lives of people today. The central importance of description in biblical theory is undeniable. The question is whether or not biblical theology stops when the description is completed.

The feeling that biblical theology cannot stop with the task of description has led to several full-scale attempts at placing the whole Old Testament under a single rubric that continues to be relevant for the community of faith. Among the organizing concepts are the covenant (W. Eichrodt), the mighty acts of God (G. E. Wright), and the elusive presence of God (S. Terrien). Other Old Testament theologians like G. von Rad have drawn attention to the central importance of continuing reflection on and recital of God's saving acts in history. Von Rad's theology is a nuanced and sophisticated version of the salvation-history approach that has been popular among Christians throughout the centuries. The chief problem with all the "single rubric" approaches is that some of the Old Testament books (e.g., Proverbs, Job, Qohelet) do not fit very well. These attempts surely focus attention on the most important parts and themes of the Old Testament, but the designation of them as theologies of the Old Testament remains problematic.

B. God's Relationship with His People

A simple introduction to the methods of Old Testament study can hardly be expected to resolve all the problems of Old Testament theology. Nevertheless, the various methods and the examples used by way of illustration in this book do point in the direction of a unifying concept for understanding the Old Testament. That unifying concept is God's relationship with his people.

In the Old Testament God is always presented with reference to his people, never as he is "in himself" in the philosophical or systematic-theological sense of that phrase. The closest thing to a list of divine attributes occurs in Exod 34:6-7: "a God merciful and gracious, slow to anger, and abounding in steadfast love and faithfulness, keeping steadfast love for thousands, forgiving iniquity..." Even in what purports to be a series of statements about the nature of God, all the phrases concern God in relationship to his people.

The people of God in the Old Testament is Israel. Are not all human beings part of God's people? Not exactly! The Bible portrays God as the creator and lord of all persons, but it also emphasizes the special quality of the relationship existing between God and Israel. In its triumphs and defeats, in its goodness and wickedness, Israel remains God's people. The New Testament writers do not deny the election of Israel to live in a unique relationship with God.

Rather, they try to show how, through Jesus the Jew of Nazareth, that unique relationship has been made available to all persons regardless of race or ethnic origin.

The Bible is the record of God's dealings with his chosen people, and the Old Testament is part of that record. As we stressed in the previous chapter, the Old Testament provides Christian faith with a vocabulary and a historical context. It reminds us that our faith is communal and historical, not simply the individual standing before God. It never lets us forget that we stand in a tradition of faith—a tradition that brings to bear on our lives God's past mighty acts on behalf of his people, that is continually being interpreted, and that shapes our response to God. This tradition is always relevant to human needs. It is always fresh. It demands an effort on our part to understand it and win our place within it.

The methods of Old Testament interpretation discussed in this book illustrate these points about the Bible as the record of God's dealing with his chosen people and about the dynamic character of Israel's tradition of faith. *Literary analysis* reveals that God dealt with his people in all areas of life (history, law, wisdom, etc.) and that the relationship was expressed in terms and literary forms that were intelligible to people at the time. *Historical criticism* reminds us that God's relationship with his people took shape over a long period of time and in a particular area of the world. It also makes us sensitive to the difference in concern between the biblical writers (interpreted history) and modern historians (objective facts). *Archaeology* unearths pertinent information about the material culture of ancient Israel and makes available ancient literary texts that can illumine parallel passages in the Bible. It too confirms the historical, this-wordly dimension of the tradition of faith.

The study of *words and motifs* shows that the richest

aspects of the tradition of faith are rooted in the experiences of God's people and that new experiences are interpreted in light of and integrated into God's covenant relationship with his chosen people. *Form criticism* unveils to us the varied ways in which that relationship is expressed (stories, laws, psalms, proverbs, prophetic oracles) and the varied settings in which the tradition was handed on before it took final written form. *Source criticism* allows us to see what blocks of written or oral material were at the disposal of the biblical writers, and *redaction criticism* enables us to get a sense of the fidelity and creativity of the final authors.

Textual criticism gives us a glimpse of how the tradition of faith has been handed on within the community for over three thousand years. Examination of recent English *translations* indicates that the process of transmission goes on and that biblical scholars and literary stylists try mightily to make accessible to more and more people the treasures of the faith. The fact that the Old Testament has been used for centuries in *worship* and continues as a major feature in services at synagogues and churches tells us that the tradition is alive and well.

The passages used in the preceding nine chapters to illustrate the various methods of interpretation also show the Old Testament to be the record of God's relationship with his people and the witness to the tradition of faith. We have seen Abraham as a model of faith in God's promise to his descendants (Gen 22:1-19), Jeremiah as an example of trust in God's promise despite the experience of destruction and exile (Jer 33:14-16), and the "famous men" of Israel's history as standing in a tradition of faith and as occasions for giving thanks to God (Sir 44:1-15).

The way in which events are handled in the Bible confirms the centrality of tradition in Israel's faith. The three accounts of the escape from Egypt in Exodus 14-15 illustrate how a story could be retold and reinterpreted at various points in Israel's history. The use of exodus imagery in Isa 40:1-11 to shed light on the return from the exile tells something important about the dynamic of Old Testament faith: It looks to the past in the effort to understand the present and then reaches beyond the present into the future. The same dynamic is present in the use of the covenant-motif to express Israel's relationship with God (Josh 24:14-15) and the reorientation of that motif in light of the destruction and exile of 587 B.C. (Jer 31:31-34).

The very process by which we are able to know anything about the heroes and events of ancient Israel adds still more dimensions to our theme of tradition. The books of the Old Testament grew out of small written and oral units of tradition (stories, laws, psalms, prophetic oracles, proverbs) that had been preserved and handed on in specific settings (royal court, the temple, schools, etc.). The content and the language of these traditions reflect the world of the ancient Near East as is shown by the light shed on the ordinances in Exod 21:23-25 from the Code of Hammurabi and certain phrases in the Psalms from the Ugaritic Baal epic. The editors or final authors of the biblical books adapted the earlier materials to the needs of their time (2 Sam 7:1-17; 1 Chr 17:1-15) and shaped the small units into complete books (Haggai).

The process of tradition did not stop when the Old Testament books reached their "canonical" form. The variant textual traditions of Deut 31:1 and 32:43 glimpsed in the Septuagint and confirmed in dramatic fashion by the discovery of the Hebrew biblical texts at Qumran bear witness both to the care with which the books were preserved and to the vitality and variety of the biblical tradition. The different English translations of Ps 46:10 and Gen 1:1-2a indicate the range of possible meanings present in two fairly simple texts and the varied ways in which those meanings are made intelligible to people today.

C. The Authority of the Old Testament

How seriously is the Old Testament to be taken by Christians, and what is its proper place in the church? Throughout the centuries it has been viewed as a pre-Christian legacy, the document of an alien religion, a set of predictions about Christ, a collection of laws, and so forth. It has been interpreted literally and allegorically. It has passed from being the Scriptures of the early church, through being a set of types or patterns of Christ and the church, to being a source for research on ancient Near Eastern history and culture.

The introduction to this volume began with ideas taken from section 12 in the Second Vatican Council's Dogmatic Constitution on Divine Revelation. Sections 14—16 of the same document consider the place of the Old Testament in the church. The Constitution insists that the books of the Old Testament were written under divine inspiration and should be received with reverence. It recommends that the Old Testament be viewed as a witness to the plan of salvation and as preparation for the coming of Christ and of the messianic kingdom. The Old Testament is said to show us true divine pedagogy and to tell us about God and humanity. The Council's discussion of the Old Testament climaxes with Augustine's saying that the New Testament lies hidden in the Old and the Old is made manifest in the New.

Each of the Constitution's efforts at expressing the role of the Old Testament in Christian faith—divine inspiration, salvation history, preparation for Christ, divine pedagogy, complement to the New Testament—has a rich history and expresses something of abiding importance. But paragraph 15 of the document also says that the books of the Old Testament contain some things that are incomplete and temporary. Which things? It is safe to presume the incomplete and temporary things include the calls for vengeance against enemies of the Psalms, the apparently devious actions of patriarchs and kings, the regulations about cultic purity and the temple, and the narrow nationalism. These incomplete and temporary things, however, add up to a fairly substantial portion of the Old Testament. Furthermore, it is hard to distinguish them from the supposedly complete and eternal aspects. The vagueness of the Council's document on this matter involves a complex of difficult problems, which cannot be resolved here.

This introduction to Old Testament exegesis has focused on the aspect of divine pedagogy, on *how* God has dealt with his chosen people. This is not the only approach to the question of the Old Testament's authority. But this approach with its emphasis on modes of communication and on specific texts allows us to listen more sensitively to those in our religious tradition who have had profound experiences in spiritual matters. Once we have understood these experiences, we can better recognize their validity and authority. The thrust of various methods of interpretation forces us to conclude that the Old Testament is best read within the community of faith and that it can enrich all who wish to stand in the tradition of faith from Abraham to the present day. An important part of earning our place within that tradition is understanding its content. This presentation of the various methods of biblical interpretation is intended as an initial step toward that goal.

Bibliography: Theology

J. Bright, *The Authority of the Old Testament* (Nashville—New York: Abingdon, 1967).

B. S. Childs, *Biblical Theology in Crisis* (Philadelphia: Westminster, 1970).

R. E. Clements, *Old Testament Theology. A Fresh Approach* (Atlanta: John Knox, 1979).

W. Eichrodt, *Theology of the Old Testament* (2 vols.; Philadelphia: Westminster, 1961-67).

A. H. J. Gunneweg, *Understanding the Old Testament* (Philadelphia: Westminster, 1978).

P.D. Hanson, *The People Called* (San Francisco: Harper & Row, 1986).

W. J. Harrington, *The Path of Biblical Theology* (Dublin: Gill & Macmillan, 1973).

G. Hasel, *Old Testament Theology: Basic Issues in the Current Debate* (Grand Rapids: Eerdmans, 1972).

J. L. McKenzie, *A Theology of the Old Testament* (Garden City, NY: Doubleday, 1974).

R.A. Oden, *The Bible Without Theology* (San Francisco: Harper & Row, 1987).

S. Terrien, *The Elusive Presence. Toward a New Biblical Theology* (New York: Harper & Row, 1978).

G. von Rad, *Old Testament Theology* (2 vols.; New York: Harper & Row, 1962-65).

G. E. Wright, *The Old Testament and Theology* (New York: Harper & Row, 1969).

W. Zimmerli, *Old Testament Theology in Outline* (Atlanta: John Knox, 1978).

POSTSCRIPT: NEW METHODS

A. Canonical Criticism

THIS PRACTICAL guide to interpreting the Old Testament has been devoted to explaining the tried and true approaches. It has deliberately avoided the novel and idiosyncratic on the ground that the basic function of the guide is to provide the information necessary for an intelligent use of the commentaries in the *Old Testament Message* series. But this restriction should not be viewed as suggesting that nothing more is to be done in refining the methods used in Old Testament study or that nothing important is developing outside of the traditional literary approaches.

One very important new development is called canonical criticism. Its most eloquent proponent is Brevard S. Childs, and its most extensive presentation is Childs's massive *Introduction to the Old Testament as Scripture*. Childs himself is unhappy with the label "canonical criticism," because it could imply that this approach simply stands beside the literary approaches of form criticism, source criticism, and redaction criticism. Canonical criticism is really a theological program that seeks to establish a stance from which the Bible can be read as Sacred Scripture. It seeks to challenge the interpreter to look closely at the biblical text in its received or canonical form and then critically to discern its function for the community of faith in the past as well as in the present and future.

The term "canon" derives from the Greek word meaning "rule" or "measure" and refers to the collection of books acknowledged as normative and authoritative by the Jewish and Christian communities of faith. The contents of the Bible constitute the canon of Scripture. The canonical critic tries to understand the peculiar shape and special function of these canonical texts. Thus the canonical critic asks two basic questions: (1) What is the theological shape of the final, canonical form of this or that book of the Old Testament? (2) What theological implications does the canonical form have for the community of faith then and now? These two questions correspond to the twofold concern of canonical criticism: theological description and actualization.

In its descriptive operation, canonical criticism parallels and indeed makes abundant use of the methods explained in this guide. Its concern with the present form of the text (the text as we now have it) is consistent with the principles of sound literary criticism, and its interest in the overall canonical shape of the book corresponds to redaction criticism conceived on the grand scale or the macroscopic level. But its focus on the theological significance of the canonical form of the book sets it apart from aesthetically oriented literary methods. Canonical criticism does not deny the need for historical criticism or for sensitivity toward the development of a text from event to words to small formal unit to source to redaction. It insists, however, that within the community of faith as the true home of the Bible the final or canonical form should have pride of place.

The book of Esther can illustrate the canonical-critical approach to Scripture. Written around 300 B.C., the book of Esther is a kind of historical novel in which the Jews are saved from the threat of total annihilation at the hands of the Persians (see 3:13) through the interventions of Queen Esther and Mordecai. It is not an obviously "religious" document in the modern understanding of that term. In fact in its Hebrew version there is not a single mention of God! But there are so many apparent "coincidences" in the story that it is possible to speak of an indirect theology according to which God works through the mediation of certain of his people.

The historical critic of the book of Esther will study it for its knowledge of Persian customs and its generally favorable attitude toward the Persian empire. The literary critic will consider the portrayal of the characters, the major motifs, the flow of the plot, and the genre of the book. The canonical critic pays particular attention to Esther 9:20-32 as supplying the reason why the book is in the canon. That passage links the account of Esther and Mordecai to the Jewish festival of Purim as its foundational story. Just as the story of the Pilgrims at Plymouth in Massachusetts provides the foundational story for the observance of Thanksgiving Day in the USA, so the story Esther and Mordecai furnished the basis for the celebration of Purim.

To the literary critic, Esther 9:20-32 appears as an appendix or an addition that contributes little to the main story. The canonical critic insists that the canonical use of the tale of Esther as the foundational story for Purim reveals what the book meant in the community of faith and why it is in the canon of Scripture. Purim emerges as the celebration of the preservation of the Jewish people, and the story of Esther and Mordecai illustrates how God works even in an indirect way to safeguard his people (see 4:13-14; 6:13). The canonical approach highlights the religious significance of the preservation of the Jewish people in an ethnic and religious sense. In the context of the canon of Scripture, the book of Esther warns against spiritualizing the concept of Israel and removing the scandal of particularity. On the other hand, the canonical approach with its sensitivity to the link between Esther and Purim and to the inclusion of the book as a whole in the believing community's canon of Scripture warns against narrow nationalism and ethnocentrism.

The strengths of the canonical-critical approach should be obvious. Its concern with the text as we now have it is sound not only on literary grounds but also on theological grounds. Its interest in the religious dimensions of the canonical forms of the books is only appropriate to the content of a collection whose primary focus is God's relationship with his people. Its attention to the canonical forms of the books within the community of faith then and now correctly refuses to separate the literature of ancient Israel from the people of Israel (and the church) and gives some very helpful suggestions as to how these ancient texts may enrich the life and practice of the believing community.

While admitting the great values of the canonical approach, I see three major problems that can be expressed in the following series of questions: Which text is canonical? Which canon should serve as the basis? Which community is the community of faith? Childs is certainly aware of these problems and offers explanations to counter each objection. Nevertheless, the objections retain their force and cast a shadow over canonical criticism as an overall theological approach to the Old Testament as Sacred Scripture.

Which text is canonical? The chapter on textual criticism drew attention to the divergent forms of the Hebrew texts of the Old Testament as seen from the discovery of the Dead Sea scrolls. The differences between the types of texts should not be exaggerated, but the fact remains that the book of Jeremiah existed at Qumran in a long edition and a short edition. The short version corresponds roughly to the Greek text of Jeremiah in the Septuagint. The Greek version of the book of Esther is somewhat longer than the Hebrew version. Even if the additions to Esther are explained as having been composed in Greek, why is the shorter, Hebrew form of the book taken to be the canonical form? In the early centuries of the Christian church, the Greek Septuagint of Jeremiah and Esther provided the "canonical" forms of the Old Testament books. Why should they now be denied canonical status in favor of the Masoretic Hebrew forms? The program of canonical criticism encounters difficulties in determining precisely which text of the Old Testament is canonical and why the Hebrew texts should necessarily be preferred to the early Greek versions.

Which canon should serve as the basis? At the very beginning of the chapter on literary criticism, there is a list of what one finds contained in the editions of the Old Testament published under the sponsorship of Jewish, Protestant, and Catholic groups. The Catholic canon includes seven more books (Tobit, Judith, 1 Maccabees, 2 Maccabees, Wisdom, Sirach, and Baruch) and somewhat longer editions of Daniel and Esther. Are these books to be denied canonical status just because their primary texts at present are in Greek? Moreover, even though both Jews and Protestants accept the same canon of Old Testament books, the order of the books in their canons is different. Yet a far more important problem is posed by the fact that Protestant Bibles include the books of the New Testament and Jewish Bibles obviously do not. For Protestants and Catholics the books of the Hebrew Bible are the Old Testament, which must be read in connection with the books of the New Testament. For Jews, these books are the Hebrew Scriptures or the Hebrew Bible, and the adjective "Old" is both irrelevant and offensive. Despite their apparent similarity, the Protestant and Jewish canons of Scripture differ.

Which community is the community of faith? Since Catholics, Protestants, and Jews have different canons of Scripture, it is not easy to be precise about how the Old Testament texts in their canonical forms are to be actualized today in the community of faith. But it is even harder to know how the canonical forms of the texts were actualized in the life of the community in antiquity. The formation of the Old Testament canon presents notoriously difficult historical problems. Childs admits that the Jewish canon was formed through a complex historical process that is largely inaccessible to critical reconstruction (p. 67). That means that we do not know exactly why these books were accepted as authoritative and not others like the now lost "Book of the Wars of the Lord" (see Num 21:14-15) and "Book of Jashar" (see Josh 10:13; 2 Sam 1:18). Were the reasons theological, historical, or apologetic? We really do not know for certain.

Which text? Which canon? Which community? These questions uncover some of the major problems connected with the theological program of canonical criticism. The practical contributions made by looking at the final forms of the Old Testament books, focusing on the religious dimensions of the texts, and reflecting on the role of the believing community vis-à-vis Scripture cannot be denied. But the theoretical difficulties raised by the different text-types, canons, and communities are substantial and will furnish ample material for debate and discussion in the coming years with regard to canonical criticism.

B. Social Sciences

The impact of the social sciences on the educational practice and the intellectual life of North America and Europe during the last fifty years has been dramatic. Today college and high-school programs generally include some exposure to the basic concepts of sociology and psychology, and many of the issues that were once the concerns of philosophers have been preempted by specialists in the social sciences. It should come as no surprise therefore that one of the most important developments in biblical studies in recent years has been the use of methods and concepts taken from the social sciences as a way of promoting increased understanding of biblical texts.

The most valuable contributions to Old Testament studies from the social sciences have been made in the areas of sociology and cultural anthropology. Attention to some of the questions customarily raised in these disciplines and to the basic concepts routinely employed in answering them has given added clarity and sophistication to processes carried out in biblical studies for many centuries.

Sociology considers the origin, development, organization, and functioning of social groups. It tries to understand and express the fundamental laws of social relations and institutions. Traditional Old Testament scholars like J. Pedersen and R. de Vaux made classic syntheses of the social realities of life in ancient Israel. But the new form of the sociological approach begun by Max Weber and represented today by N. K. Gottwald, R. P. Carroll, and P. D. Hanson asks sociological questions and uses sociological models in answering them. It asks about the social status and ideological concerns of the characters or groups in the texts, the points of contention or struggle, the ways in which the conflicts are resolved, and the present-day analogies.

For example, Gottwald describes Israel's social structure between 1250 and 1050 B.C. as a deliberate and highly conscious "retribalization" process in which "the religion of Yahweh was a crucial societal instrument for cementing and motivating the peculiar constellation of unifying and decentralizing sociocultural patterns necessary to the optimal functioning of the social system and, *in extremis,* to the sheer survival of the system (p. xxiii)." In other words, Gottwald is mainly interested in the social function played by religion in the earliest history of Israel. Carroll explores the phenomenon of unfulfilled and reinterpreted prophecies in ancient Israel and the inclusion of such prophecies in the canon of Scripture. He explains it in light of the concept of cognitive dissonance—the process by which people gradually accept and assimilate experiences that initially seem to contradict their deepest convictions. Thus the process of reinterpretation that is so characteristic of the Old Testament is explained by reference to a process that every person and group undergoes at some time and on which an ample sociological literature exists. Hanson analyzes various efforts at restoring Judaism after the Exile as a clash between the hieratic (priestly and temple-centered) and the visionary (prophetic) mentalities, and interprets them in light of the intellectual tools developed by social scientists and secular historians.

Cultural anthropology is closely related to sociology and includes within its scope linguistics, ethnography, ethnology, and archaeology. Its central insight is that culture communicates. Any cultural event (a banquet, a wedding, a lecture, a football game, a concert, etc.) conveys a good deal of information, often unconsciously, about those who participate. That information goes far beyond the menu or the content of the lecture or the final score of the game. The cultural event is always part of a complicated system of relationships, and the behavior of the participants can reveal their deepest assumptions about the world and their place in it. The task of the cultural anthropologist is to describe as accurately as possible the cultural events that take place in a society and to decode the messages embedded in them. Special attention is given to the logic by which the symbols presented in the cultural events are connected.

The most effective way to do cultural anthropology is by means of on-the-site observation. Cultural anthropology usually demands field-work. It is necessary to enter the other culture, understand and describe the various cultural rituals (eating, marrying, worshipping, etc.), and lay bare the whole system that underlies these events. It is obviously not possible to apply to the Old Testament the sophisticated techniques of firsthand observation that are employed by cultural anthropologists in the field. But the basic concerns of the cultural anthropologists (cultural events or rituals as revelatory of a whole system of beliefs, and the interconnectedness of symbols) have made an impact on the study of the Bible.

In the nineteenth century, Old Testament study was given something of a new lease on life by the Western rediscovery of Near Eastern or oriental cultures. Travellers quickly observed parallels between the customs of people in the Near East and what was described in the Old Testament. In many cases such observations were enlightening, but in other instances they were superficial and ultimately confusing. The new form of the cultural-anthropological study of the Old Testament is at once more cautious in reaching for analogies from outside the Bible and at the same time more adventurous in its explanations of what this or that phenomenon reveals about ancient Israel's world-view.

The best contributions to Old Testament study by cultural anthropologists have occurred in areas that are usually neglected by modern readers. For example, Mary Douglas has attempted a comprehensive interpretation of the dietary rules found in Deut 14:3-20 and Lev 11:2-42. Rejecting the hygienic, allegorical, and historical-religious explanations of why some animals are considered clean and others are forbidden, she discovers underlying these very detailed and complicated rules a concept of holiness as completeness and order. Holiness requires that creatures conform to their classes and different classes of animals should not be confused. Holiness means keeping distinct the categories of creation. Cloven-hoofed, cud-chewing ungulates are the "proper" kinds of food, and therefore it is forbidden to eat the camel (not cloven-hoofed) and the pig (not cud-chewing). In the water, scaly fish swim with fins; anything that does not have scales and fins is unclean. Four-footed creatures that fly are unclean, and so are the creatures having two legs and two hands but going on all four like quadrupeds. In ancient Israel, according to anthropologist Douglas, the dietary laws functioned as signs able to inspire meditation on the oneness, purity, and completeness of God.

An approach to literary texts that developed out of cultural anthropology and modern linguistics is called structuralism. It seeks first of all to clarify the surface structure of the text and in this respect is akin to literary criticism. But the real focus of attention is directed to the underpinning of each complex of biblical texts. These deep structures are the fundamental assumptions about the world and about life that generate the surface structures in the texts. The major concepts of structuralism include the following: language as a code or a system, the discovery of meaning in the interaction between the signifier and the signified, the binary oppositions or contrasts within the system (raw/cooked, up/down, full/empty), the static side of language at a specified point in time (synchrony) as opposed to the historical development (diachrony), the distinction between the syntagmatic (horizontal or linear) and paradigmatic (vertical) dimensions, and the mental processes by which texts are generated.

These brief explanations of the new forms of sociological and cultural-anthropological approaches to the Old Testament illustrate some of the positive contributions to our understanding of specific passages. These approaches bring in a new set of questions and concerns, and thus they open up the possibility of discovering aspects of the text that may have previously gone unnoticed. They also speak the language and use the methods that are increasingly prominent in the study of religion today. Finally, their "social" orientation is especially appropriate to the study of a religious literature mainly concerned with peoples and groups and only rarely interested in individual psychology.

These explanations also illustrate some of the problems involved in using the social sciences in biblical study. The social sciences tend to get lost in their own jargon and thus make simple things very complicated, as the quotation from Gottwald and the list of structuralist concepts show. Also, on account of the long historical distance between the composition of the Old Testament books and the present day, it is necessary to adapt seriously or at least nuance carefully the scientific techniques of empirical observation employed by sociologists and cultural anthropologists. Finally, the social sciences purport to be value-free or at least assume the stance of the neutral observer rather than that of the active participant. The sociologist or the anthropologist stands off from the group, observes the group from the outside, and tries to describe and explain the social interactions. If God enters into the description, it is only in terms of what the members of the group might say about God. Social science is not (and does not claim to be) theology. Its concerns and concepts may well enrich our theology, but they cannot substitute for it.

Bibliography: New Methods

R. P. Carroll, *When Prophecy Failed: Cognitive Dissonance in the Prophetic Traditions of the Old Testament* (New York: Seabury, 1979).

B. S. Childs, *Introduction to the Old Testament as Scripture* (Philadelphia: Fortress, 1979).

R. de Vaux, *Ancient Israel. Volume 1: Social Institutions; Volume 2: Religious Institutions* (New York—Toronto: McGraw-Hill, 1961).

M. Douglas, *Purity and Danger: An Analysis of Concepts of Pollution and Taboo* (London—Henley: Routledge & Kegan Paul, 1966).

N. K. Gottwald, *The Tribes of Yahweh. A Sociology of the Religion of Liberated Israel 1250-1050 B.C.E.* (Maryknoll, NY: Orbis, 1979).

P. D. Hanson, *The Dawn of Apocalyptic. The Historical and Sociological Roots of Jewish Apocalyptic Eschatology* (rev. ed.; Philadelphia: Fortress, 1979).

E. Leach, *Culture and Communication. The Logic by which Symbols are Connected. An Introduction to the Use of Structuralist Analysis in Social Anthropology* (Cambridge: Cambridge University Press, 1976).

D. Patte, *What Is Structural Exegesis?* (Philadelphia: Fortress, 1976).

J. Pedersen, *Israel, Its Life and Culture* (4 vols.; London: Oxford University Press, 1926-40).

J.A. Sanders, *Canon and Community: A Guide to Canonical Criticism* (Philadelphia: Fortress, 1984).

J. A. Sanders, *Torah and Canon* (Philadelphia: Fortress, 1972).

P. Trible, *Texts of Terror* (Philadelphia: Fortress, 1984).

M. Weber, *Ancient Judaism* (Glencoe, IL: Free Press, 1952).

R.R. Wilson, *Sociological Approaches to the Old Testament* (Philadelphia: Fortress, 1984).

Appendix
Questions in Exegesis

1. *Literary Criticism*

   What words, images, and symbols appear?

   What characters appear, and what is the progress of thought?

   What literary form does the text have?

   How does the form contribute to expressing the content?

2. *Historical Criticism*

   What really happened?

3. *Parallels*

   What elements do the two texts have in common, and at what points do they differ or contradict one another?

   What is the historical relationship between the two texts?

4. *Word Study*

   Where else does the word appear, and what does it mean there?

   What meaning does it have in this context?

   Where does this instance stand in the term's history?

5. *Form Criticism*

   What is the literary form of the text?
   What does the literary form tell about the history of the community?

6. *Source Criticism*

   Did the document being studied have a source?
   What did that source say?
   How has the author used the source?

7. *Redaction Criticism*

   What unique views or unusual emphases does the author place on the sources?
   What is the author's life situation and theological outlook?

8. *Textual Criticism*

   Are there ancient variant readings?
   What can be explained away as unconscious or conscious alterations?
   What reading is demanded by the context, language, and style of the document?

9. *Modern Translations*

   What Hebrew, Aramaic, or Greek text underlies the translation?
   What decisions did the translators have to make?
   What philosophy of translation is operative?
   Has anything been lost in translation?

10. *Meaning (Hermeneutics)*

    What does the text say?
    What do we bring to the text?
    What does it mean today?